WHEN YOU
MEAN BUSINESS
ABOUT
YOURSELF

When You
Mean Business
About
Yourself

Ray Capp

Rutledge Hill Press®
Nashville, Tennessee

A Division of Thomas Nelson, Inc.
www.ThomasNelson.com

Published by Rutledge Hill Press, a Thomas Nelson company, P.O. Box 141000, Nashville, Tennessee 37214.

Library of Congress Cataloging-in-Publication Data

Capp, Ray, 1953-
When you mean business about yourself / Ray Capp.
    p. cm.
    ISBN 1-55853-948-4
    1. Success—Psychological aspects. 2. Success in business. 3. Role playing.
I. Title.
BF637.S8 C37 2002
158.1—dc21   2002001222

Printed in the United States of America

02 03 04 05—5 4 3 2 1

To

Diane Capp, my wife,

without whom I would have

missed out on most of the

best lessons in this business of life.

Table of Contents

ACKNOWLEDGMENTS

This book has taken a considerable amount of work putting together. I am deeply indebted to my wife, Diane, who has helped me significantly over the years as I first put my ideas and thoughts onto paper. Without her none of this would be possible. I am grateful to my publisher, Larry Stone, who decided to take on the project, to my editors, Tom Wood and Geoff Stone, who brought my thoughts into focus and kept me on track, and to Bryan Curtis and his team who got the word out about my book.

INTRODUCTION

During the past several decades of my life in corporate America, I have seen the ravages of inflation, foreign competition, the oil embargo, declining productivity, and the stock market travails of 1989. The greatest period of capital expansion in the history of the world has been accompanied by wildly fluctuating currencies, heightened consumerism, the burst of the Internet bubble, and the whipsaw ride taken to explore the frontiers of the global economy.

Successful businesses have survived all of the challenges engendered by these market phenomena (and most of the medicines administered by corporate witch doctors trying to cure the ailments) and are thriving today as a happy testimony to their hardiness and resilience. The good news is that all of these survival skills are transferable, learnable, practicable, and applicable to you and the challenges you face in your life experiences.

People have a lot to learn from the way businesses conduct themselves. Companies are very deliberate about their productivity, resource utilization, and planning. Most of us continue to search for ways to improve in these areas. We must recognize that corporations face the same world we do and the better ones have developed effective responses that can be adopted by anyone wishing to improve his personal lot in life.

In this book, I will review the many discoveries successful businesses have come to embrace as a result of their painful passages and outline how I think individuals can capitalize on this learning to advance their goals, objectives, self-understanding, success, and happiness.

Both you and Exxon will fail to achieve your objectives if you disappoint those who rely on you. Neither Disney nor you will be successful if you behave in ways that are inconsistent with what is expected of you. And, just as Microsoft must continually seek new products, you must constantly seek new ways to achieve a return on the investments you make of your time, energy, and heart. Don't let any preconceived notions you have about business being big, bad, calculating, or impersonal stand in your way of identifying with its problems, its opportunities, and its methods for dealing with them. The payoffs must be sufficient for both business and us as individuals to risk and commit our resources—for neither corporate nor personal resources will ever be as ample as we would like.

The better, more successful companies know that it's the human side of their enterprises that makes them go, and my studies of business and the business of life lead me to the conclusion that success ultimately boils down to the long-term ability to understand people and how they behave while they go about getting what they want. It's about building long-term relationships that lead to the rewards in life. The payoffs can come in dollars or love; the efficiency comes from not having to start over every day in life, like the crooked snake oil salesman of legend who continuously gets run out of the town on a rail.

In the stage play, *Camelot,* Merlin the Magician had a way of teaching the young King Arthur his lessons by turning him into a bird. It was good for the monarch to gain an understanding of life from a fresh point of view. Of course the lad knew how to live, but to *think* about how to live and to see how others did things from this lofty vantage point was good magic indeed. The restrictions of his previous earthbound perspective vanished. He learned and grew as he saw things differently.

Let's examine some successful businesses to see what they see, to think how they've thought, and to discover what we can learn from their stories.

WHEN YOU
MEAN BUSINESS
ABOUT
YOURSELF

One

ALL YOUR WORLDS ARE STAGES: KNOW YOUR ROLES

There's more than one you—
so adapt to your audiences.

You have heard it before, "It's just a stage you're going through." Stop and think about this sentence with fresh eyes. Think about who you are now, while you keep in mind all that the word "stage" can mean. For instance, you have reached a certain stage in your life. Obviously, we're talking here about the step-by-step procession of life stages we all pass through, what Shakespeare called the "seven ages" between birth and death. But the word has another meaning as well, and every day you step on to a stage in yet another Shakespearean sense: you're standing in the footlights, and your cue is coming. "All the world's a stage, and all the men and women merely players," goes the famous speech from *The Merchant of Venice*. "They have their exits and their entrances; and one man in his time plays many parts."

As you interact with the people in your life, the roles you play each day continuously define who you are. You present yourself one way in one situation and another way in another situation. We think of a person who is "two-faced" as someone who is false or hypocritical—

but actually, each of us may have five or ten faces we present to the world at different moments in our day. Hopefully, all these different personas in some way reflect the real people inside us.

In the corporate world, where I have spent my adult life, big companies routinely present different "faces"—brand names or business units—to different customers. To do this effectively, they must manage their roles. You, too, can manage your roles with different people in different situations. In fact, everything else I'm going to say in this book flows from one principle: *Manage your roles, and you can manage your life*. Learn the expected lines, practice the steps, and believe in the various characters you're going to portray, and you will excel. Life is the stage, and if you apply the good business practices described in this book, you can be the star of the show!

❧

KNOWING YOUR ROLE

Successful businesses play different roles in different markets. You should know the role you are playing at any given moment and play that role to the hilt.

To be successful in your life's roles, you must continually make adjustments in how you present yourself. Each role will have its own unique demands. For instance, the skills used to achieve a successful marriage are far different than those used to achieve success at work. You will have many other roles as well—teacher, friend, boss, subordinate, neighbor, parent, child, and so on. Each of these relationships cries out for a separate set of behaviors and skills—and you must adapt yourself accordingly.

The business world demands this same flexibility. For example, the General Electric Company (GE) includes thirteen separate businesses, which could each independently be ranked in the Fortune 500. GE honcho Jack Welch, who retired in 2001, became successful at the helm of a corporation that sells dishwashers, aircraft engines, NBC television advertising, computer timesharing, nuclear medicine cameras, home mortgages, and light bulbs. Welch and his team ran not a single company but a network of world-class organizations, each going toe-to-toe with the toughest competitors in its own line of business.

For each of GE's units, the customer base, the rules of the road, and the standards of performance are specific to that particular industry. One set of managerial virtues has enabled GE to produce a locomotive in twenty-six days instead of the ninety-two days it took in 1993.

> QUALITY IS NOT A SINGLE THING BUT AN AURA, AN ATMOSPHERE, AN OVERPOWERING FEELING THAT A COMPANY IS DOING EVERYTHING WITH EXCELLENCE.
> —JACK WELCH

A completely different set of skills and attributes has enabled GE's Structured Finance Group to put together over a trillion dollars worth of corporate investment deals in the last five years. Clearly, GE defines success differently in different realms—and I can guarantee you Welch understood he couldn't expect his choo-choo people to operate the same way his TV people did.

How can you run your life with the efficiency and success that Welch displayed at GE? First of all, you have to learn to be successful with different kinds of people in different kinds of situations.

Figure out what it is you alone have to offer. Tailor your actions to maximize your chances of stardom on each particular stage on which you play. Target your efforts to elicit the best possible reaction from the crowd you serve. This doesn't mean you're being hypocritical; it simply means you're determining the needs and characteristics of each sphere you enter. There's nothing wrong with adjusting your behavior here and there to create a good impression. To be successful at this, however, you have to ask a lot of questions—and then be willing to act on the answers.

Here's an example: Let's say that after ten years as a homemaker, you're looking to go back to the salaried life. You have sought out a clerical position, a job for which you know you have ample credentials. Before you go for your job interview, you need to be sure you understand the qualities the company will be seeking in an applicant. This means you won't go into your interview talking about how you love kids or explaining your deep faith in God. These two things may both be true—and they may be important aspects of who you are—but as worthy as these qualities are, they don't pertain to the stage on which you're playing. Instead, you'll want to make crystal clear how your personal integrity and your experience as a household manager qualify you to keep track of your would-be department's budget.

This approach doesn't ask you to deny your love for your kids; in fact, you may be taking this job just so you can pay for your children's college education. You don't have to deny your faith either; but be aware that religion is not correlated to clerical accuracy in the minds of most supervisors. You'll have a chance, if you ever get off first base, to express yourself in all your splendid complexity to these people. But first you need to establish a relationship with them. And in order to do that, you need to market the product they want to buy.

This is not hypocrisy. You are still a religious child lover! You can't and shouldn't deny your true nature. But you absolutely must play to your audience—and this means you determine the group of skills that audience needs, and then you present those skills in their best possible light. If you don't, people will simply "fill in the blanks" for you. In other words, your audience will infer your qualities and skills based on what you tell them about yourself—and you will have given them control of your most valuable asset: your reputation.

A job interview is just one example of how you might need to adjust your behavior and presentation for a particular audience. You have many roles in your life, and each is unique. Just as GE expects its light bulb business to produce something different from its small-appliance ventures, you have to play each role within its own context.

Obvious, you say? Sure it is—while you sit there reading. But go out and see how the world lives. Many companies do very poor jobs when it comes to handling their various business units' unique needs. These companies often expect the same reports, the same programs, and the same information across the board. This is lunacy. Different businesses thrive exactly *because* of their specific strengths and unique ways of serving their marketplaces. An attempt to make businesses all look the same takes away the very peculiarities that lead to success. And people are no different.

<hr />

DEFINING YOUR RELATIONSHIPS

Successful businesses define their markets to best meet their needs. You should define your relationships so you, too, will know what to expect.

When toy maker Mattel Inc. promoted Jill E. Barad to the role of chief executive officer, the move looked visionary. After all, Barad had built a sterling reputation as a strategic marketing whiz with the Barbie doll line, and now she was shattering the "glass ceiling" that has historically limited women's access to the executive suite. But then the whispers started coming from people at Mattel. The rap was that Barad did not seem as obsessed with her company's vital numbers as Wall Street expects of a CEO these days. That sounds like a solvable problem, and it might have been. There were other blind spots, however—or so reported the *New York Times* in a 1999 profile. Barad, the paper said, had "fundamentally failed to address high executive turnover, focused too much on the saturated Barbie brand, and is rumored not to listen very well to well-intended employees or customers who try to be helpful. The Company is hurting." Barad resigned in February 2000. She had failed to meet the unique needs of her new position.

This sad tale makes me think of *The Wizard of Oz*. Remember the man behind the curtain? When an angry Dorothy discovers the Wiz is not what he seems and declares him to be a "very bad man," he sets her straight: "Oh, no my dear, I am a very good man—just a very bad wizard." Nothing says you can't be both a man and a wizard—but you have to know exactly when you are acting in which role. Otherwise, like the poor old Wiz, you'll find that no matter how good you are in one role, you'll still fail in the other.

Besides, neither a human being nor a corporation can be good at everything. And neither one should try to be. Success is highly specific to certain competencies in certain circumstances for which there is a limited demand. In our culture, we expect winners to be good at everything—that cannot be. Each of us must be aware of our limitations. Oz was a truly pathetic wizard. He should never have been operating in that capacity. In the end, he wisely disengaged himself from the role to the betterment of all.

In the 1960s, by virtue of what we now call the "conglomerate ethic" an assertion was made that a good executive was qualified to manage any kind of operation. While this may be true, at the time the theory was misapplied. Executives were trying to manage different companies following the same formula, demanding similar reports, filling out the same forms, and using the same ratios. Such thinking is not so popular today because a single management team is seldom capable of being sophisticated enough to treat each subordinate company the way the distinct marketplace demands. Different businesses need to have the freedom to operate using different numeric goals and financial ratios. Good managers understand this and don't treat all businesses the same. A better approach is for a company to articulate different measures of success for every business it runs. This is what Jack Welch did with relish.

By the same token, you need to evaluate each of the roles you play. Why are you playing a particular role in the first place? What are your psychic, emotional, spiritual, or financial payoffs? Are you using the appropriate skills and methods to achieve those payoffs? The best relationships are founded on intense, unique, and highly specific ways of interacting.

Remember this because it's tough to accept. Unfortunately, once we find a "good" relationship, we often try to fill all our needs through that single avenue. And once we find successful ways of relating to someone, we tend to use these same techniques with the rest of the people in our lives, regardless of the relationship or personal preferences. Of course, this is a very convenient way of living. It's very simple. But it's also terribly unproductive. Accountants in those big conglomerates might prefer if every unit reported its results on the same forms—but how many customers buy a company's products because the accountants at headquarters are happy? And how many people in your world will be satisfied with what you have to offer if you serve it up exactly the same for everyone?

I've seen a big-time executive barking orders at home and a highly paid attorney cross-examining family members in public. These guys haven't grasped the fact that the very skills that bring them esteem in the boardroom or courtroom bring only resentment and alienation when deployed among family and friends. You can't treat everybody the same. It won't work. And yet people and companies continue to assume that if they are winners in one arena using a specific set of behaviors, they can replicate that achievement in a separate environment by using the same behaviors.

Unfortunately, if you get locked into the skills that brought you success in one field, you often find yourself singularly unsuccessful elsewhere. Some roles and some businesses simply don't mix. For instance, boutique customers expect personalized service, beautiful displays, and well-dressed employees. At a sand and gravel pit, however, the employees are expected to dress grungy, and how many ways can you personalize gravel delivery? You cannot run a boutique the way you run a sand and gravel pit. And even within the same business, different roles demand different ways of presenting yourself.

Internally, within your psyche, don't mix business with your personal life. If your job enables you to work at home, don't spend the day in your pajamas; get up, clean up, and dress up. Go to a workspace reserved for this kind of activity and mentally remove yourself from Home Sweet Home. This also means: Don't answer the home phone.

You're not there to buy aluminum siding for your house—or chat with your best friend.

Do everything you can to reduce the spillover of anxiety and stress from one role to another. It won't help your home life one iota if you yell at your secretary because the kids are driving you crazy. On the other hand, when your workday ends, empty your mind of messy business matters; the kids need you to pay attention to them. Later, when you are alone with your spouse, you can talk about what's troubling you at work.

It should be clear to you by now that if you're an accountant, you shouldn't nit-pick the family budget. The converse is also true but less obvious: an accountant shouldn't spend his lunch hours shopping for paint for the new family room. To mix your work responsibilities with your home responsibilities asks you to switch your thought processes—and that uses unnecessary mental energy. Instead, use lunchtime to further your business career, and use your weekends for family business, keeping things segregated to the greatest practical extent.

And if you're finding it too tough to "wind down" after a hard day's work, maybe you should loosen your tie on the way home. Other commuters don't care if you look "impressive." Change your clothes when you walk in the door. Our attire is linked to what we think about ourselves—and what we think about ourselves drives our behavior.

The fewer role switches in a day, the better. This is hard to do and sometimes impossible, but you can still aim for this as your ideal. Make a habit of knowing what role you are in at a particular moment and act in that role, intensely. Switch when necessary, but do so as infrequently as you can. This conserves energy. Hardly anyone I know can achieve this all the time, but it's worth a try. Try to "live in the moment"; be conscious of the role you're playing currently. It gets tricky because we all have so many roles and lead such compartmentalized lives.

⤫

PRIORITIZING YOUR ROLES

Successful businesses develop a hierarchy of roles that should be articulated and understood. You, too, must prioritize the roles in your life.

Certain businesses are in the corporate portfolio for specific reasons that can be ordered. This is obvious in a turn-around situation when management will identify a viable core business that must be defended and guarded at all costs. This business will be the piece that will grow into the company's future, while other businesses will be sold off, milked, or developed. The fate of each business segment depends on its position in the hierarchy of roles.

The Catholic Church, successful if for no other reason than that it has survived for twenty centuries, is very clear about its priorities. The church's hierarchy reinforces the organization's goals. It has been skillful over the years in starving out projects with low potential return and feeding those initiatives more in line with the priorities of "top management."

This same principle means that as an individual you should frequently rethink how you have organized the major roles in your life. This is part of the painful process we call maturing.

At the corporate level, maturing means a business doesn't take it personally when a sister division uses up more corporate cash. That's just how it is. You both want it, only one can have it, and the corporation, in advancing one business venture over another, sends significant signals about the role each business is expected to play in the scheme of things. Some can block, some will tackle. On the personal level, this means when your wife takes on a new profession outside the home, you accept the new distribution of family time and resources. You understand there will be payoffs—as well as a price to pay. You don't whine because your wife no longer has time to bake your favorite chocolate chip cookies.

Maturing also means that when children fight over the roles their parents ask them to play, parents handle their complaints firmly. Immaturity asks that all be given the same priority. In real life, there are different tasks to be accomplished and different roles to play if the family entity is to make progress. Each must play his or her unique role—which means that family members will all have separate responsibilities. As a "family manager," you will help all members of the "corporation" understand their own positions in the family dynamic. This applies to you as well. If you do not understand your own role and the part you play in the whole, you are likely to exhibit some very unusual behaviors. Know your place. You are valuable for that role. Don't get confused about who you are or what you are there to be doing.

A successful business must do the same thing. For instance, custodial accountants and their ilk tend to be the scorekeepers. After the business results are played out, they look into their ledgers and tell us what happened. Management has a critical need for them to keep their books. But the best companies demand that no one ever stops or even slows down the revenue-producing activities just so that someone else can keep score. Bookkeeping should never interfere with the actual work to be done. The game of business does not stop for the scorekeepers.

Inside a business organization, there are also staff support organizations. These are there to make the moneymaking people more effective and efficient, not the other way around. I once worked in a company where the accounts receivable manager thought that the whole company was there so that he could evaluate the credit-worthiness of prospective accounts. He was obviously misguided.

Business firms set priorities by first drawing up a strategy for each business. Strategic planning has received a lot of press over the years, but I think it's easiest to understand it as a series of prioritized decisions made up in advance. You decide the really big issues up front. Then, when you confront a sticky situation, you will have already thought out, calmly, how you should respond. These decisions are arrayed in a hierarchy, and the rules that come out of the whole process are more than ample to guide a business—or a life—over time. Everyone knows that at Ford, for example, "Quality is Job One." If there is a decision to be made between compromising quality and reducing a department's scrap rate this month, all the supervisors and employees are encouraged to go for the quality. "If you take care of quality," says Ford, "profitability and job security will follow."

A successful company also develops a diverse customer base so that no single group of customers can exert undue influence over it. At the same time that companies bend over backward to serve their customers, they also organize to avoid becoming hostage to those customers' demands. It's a dangerous business practice to depend totally on one market. As an individual, anytime you rely largely on one source of emotional support, you're playing an equally risky game.

What's more, if you develop a variety of useful roles around a central theme in your life, you're more balanced as a person. You gain perspective. Things sort themselves out because you have a greater sense of what's really important. You have points of reference . . . and with them comes greater control. You don't have to sweat the small stuff, as they say. And who wants to be a small-stuff-sweater, anyway?

In your own life, you need to know not only what roles are being acted out and when, but also which ones are the most important. This knowledge will be based on decisions you've made in advance. It is important to be a clown—be playful with the kids—but when your kids ask for help with their homework or need to be punished, that is the time to be their parent. Everything else will derive from this set of priorities. Throw your heart into your roles—and don't be surprised when other people act out theirs. Accept that you can't live long with the same set of roles. Actively seek new ones with richer payoffs. Understand that other people will too. Develop a "hierarchy of roles" you can use to establish priorities and resolve conflicts between roles. And be sure to divest yourself of any old, unproductive roles so that those remaining will work together with one another. Prioritize what's central to your life so that when the inevitable conflicts arise, placing critical demands on your energies, you have a mechanism in place that clearly helps you to *do the most important thing*.

～

MANAGING YOUR ROLES

Successful businesses coordinate their various roles. You should manage your roles to clarify your relationships.

One of the most difficult aspects of developing role sophistication may be the challenge of dealing with the person with whom you have more than one role. You know the person who is both your boss and your friend, your spouse who is your business partner, the teacher who is your next-door neighbor. In these situations, neither of you may be clear as to which hat you are wearing. It can get complicated. Be up front about it. Talk about it. Make some rules to protect the soft underbelly of your relationship. Get it worked out—or it will work you over.

Practice role sophistication devoutly. The mistakes and travails associated with hiring friends are legion. Don't do it. Nor should you borrow money from them or necessarily even patronize their businesses. You cannot easily say "no" in any of these situations. It produces the worst kind of mess. Friendship's responsibilities often take precedence over those of the role that has you there in the first place. Try to avoid this situation. If you are out shopping in your role as a business executive or homemaker, then friendship has little to do with the reason you need the goods. So go where you would go if your friend weren't in the business. This doesn't mean that you don't ever buy from her. It only means that you go to the place that most benefits the role in which you are operating at the time you are making purchase decisions.

Now, the "friend" in you still wishes this proprietor the best, but the professional buyer in you may make a determination that there's a better buy. So, send your friend a copy of an article you read that may benefit her establishment. Discuss the deal you got down the street. The input will help her in her business. If the friendship means anything, you can drop in the next time to see if the situation has changed. Make sure your friends know how you are about this sort of thing. It can be very disconcerting to be friends with some people because they expect you to support them in all their activities and endeavors, even those that have nothing to do with the friendship. Be careful of people who expect you to be "true blue, do-or-die" friends. They'll be upset if you don't cosign their loan, when all you wanted was someone you could count on for doubles once a week.

Don't misread my message. Respect for different roles and their demands should not be taken to mean, "business always comes first." In order to coordinate a corporation's various roles, it must have a plan for *each* business. And it is absolutely critical for you to have a plan for each role in your life. Otherwise, you may find that important roles in your life are ignored as you allow yourself to become a slave to the demands of other roles. This is where the importance of prioritizing your roles comes into play.

Many high-powered executives subordinate their personal lives to their professional ones to such an extent that their lives are sadly out of balance. Their folly often goes undetected until a moment of personal tragedy strikes—when it becomes painfully clear that roles other than that of "executive" are significant sources of their identities. If a spouse dies, how important is professional achievement?

If a relationship is vital to a successful company, that company attends to it. Develop all your important relationships, too. Of course, some are more essential to your future than others. Corporations also deal with that circumstance.

⁓

RECOGNIZING OTHERS' NEEDS

Successful businesses understand the varying needs of each market. You, too, should understand that for every role you have, your fellow players have distinctly different needs.

Fail to meet customer expectations, and you won't be in business for long. You can get away with failure to give consumers exactly what they *want* on occasion, but there's no wiggle room for giving them what they *expect*. And so it goes in real life, off the clock. The people in your life will all have expectations of you, just as you will have expectations of them. Your life will be frustrating indeed if you expect your friends to be your surrogate parents or your boss to be your teacher. Define in your own mind the roles being played by those around you. What are the expectations that go along with those roles? The secret of role sophistication comes down to knowing which hat you have on at the moment—and acting consciously in the interests of that role. That means you determine exactly what those around you expect from you as you play your part—and then you do your best to adjust your behaviors accordingly.

Grocery stores don't make much money on sugar, flour, and many other staples. These products were downgraded to commodities long ago—but a whole generation of store owners has been forced to stock the stuff just because shoppers can't imagine a grocery store without them. People would be outraged if they were told that the grocer's overhead structure would not permit profitable distribution of these foods. Can you imagine the poor grocery clerk who had to tell her customers to head for the feed-and-grain store if they wanted flour, where they'd have to buy a fifty-pound sack?

The people in your life are not that different from grocery store customers. Some activities in your life may not seem personally profitable or fulfilling; but you still have to cut your grass, go to Mary's recital, and shine your shoes. It's the price you must continue to pay for the roles in life you've chosen to pursue. This price is what we call having responsibilities.

You can't avoid these less than pleasurable chores—but you can do everything you can to resolve conflicts between your roles and their responsibilities. Many companies have divested themselves of profitable operations that somehow don't fit their corporate culture. These businesses tend to do better when they're spun off to an outfit that appreciates them and the market forces that drive them. You can do the same in your life. Some roles and their responsibilities, while profitable at one level, may demand from you more energy than they are worth, energy that might better be spent on other roles in your life. Take time to evaluate the roles you play. Be willing to divest yourself of roles whose responsibilities conflict with what is most important to you.

Either meet the expectations of the role you are in—or get out of it. People expect you to act appropriately for each role you play. If you are the boss, don't become an active participant in office gossip. Yes, keep plugged in. Use the grapevine to test ideas and provide feedback, but don't stand around the proverbial water cooler. People will resent you if you don't act your role. If you depend on these people for your payoffs in life . . . look out. Folks want you to play the role they see you in. They are uncomfortable if they see you act otherwise. This is a very potent concept. The rewards are there for you if you abide by the ground rules. And the penalties loom large for transgressors. If you are a minister, teacher, or some other public leader, you cannot run around on your spouse in public and get away with it. Society will ask you to choose. You cannot run a hospital that promotes humanitarianism while it turns away all indigents. The community won't tolerate it. For each role you play, be aware of your audience's expectations.

Ninety percent of human activity in most interactions can be predicted. Don't get so caught up in the activity of the moment that you lose sight of that ratio. You're a doctor examining a very sick child. How do you expect the mother to act? You're a supplier to a domestic auto manufacturer. How do you think the purchasing people will relate to you—on quality? or on price? Expect people to behave in their roles. If you understand the roles of those with whom you share significant relationships, you may be able to develop solutions to their problems before they are even able to articulate the problem itself. Don't expect the same solutions to match the expectations of all the "marketplaces" in your life.

Somewhere down the road from where you live, I'm sure you could find a guy who lays asphalt paving for his living. If you talked to this guy, you'd find that the particulars of selling asphalt paving to homeowners for their driveways are different from those required for bidding on a new section of road for the county. The bid process, the payment terms, the lead time, and the price are all tailored for these two customers of this one business. This guy is into what you'd call two market segments. Yes, he's delivering basically the same product, but it is advertised, sold, installed, and warranted differently. Across America, today and everyday, anyone who expects to be in business this time next year must understand that different sets of customers must be treated in unique ways.

Businesspeople must also treat the different segments of their companies differently. Smart bosses have learned the hard way that they can't treat all employees the same. They must treat them all equally well, but that's not the same as treating them all the same. Some people are motivated by money, others by title, access to information, status, and so on.

Again, these same principles apply to life outside the office. For instance, parents can benefit from this flexible approach as they deal with their developing children; because Susie will work hard for a bag of peanuts does not mean that Joey will be even remotely motivated by the same payoff. Parents who insist on treating each child the same, using what appears at first glance to be a "fair" program of similar activities and rewards, actually end up treating some of their children very shabbily. In fact, parents may damage their relationships with their children. Instead, these parents need to look for the unique qualities of each child. In the same way a successful business seeks to tailor its approach to a key account, parents can develop creative ways to stimulate their separate relationships with each of their children.

Take a look at your life. Do you find yourself repeating the same behavior patterns in all your life roles? Are you are married to certain activities? Forget them. Learn new ones. Nurture and grow relationships, not a set of behaviors. Embrace flexibility, and your life and that of the others will be fresher, more fun, and more rewarding.

UNDERSTANDING POTENTIAL

Successful businesses know that all market segments will not react the same. Likewise, you should know that each of your roles will react differently when presented with change.

A business may sell patio glasses to K-Mart, stainless steel cups to the government, and coffee mugs to Spiegel. If it announces a change in the basic unit of measure from one cup to 250 milliliters, one of these three may take credit for the idea and buy more. One might have to go to committee and effectively stop any activity on the item for eighteen months, and one might not care one way or another. The business is dealing with three different markets, and each will react in its own way. You can bank on a department store reacting differently from a mass merchant. The government is sure to respond in ways the specialty catalogs would never imagine.

By the same token, the executive in you may be thrilled at the prospects of the job offer in Hoboken. The mother in you may be torn apart. The spouse in you may not care either way. These different reactions are probably caused by the responses of those in your life. Will all the people in your life feel the same way about your major announcement? Well, of course not, because all the significant "others" in your life relate to you on a different basis. You had better figure out the best way (and correct order) in which to put the news across to those in your life. For some of these people, it better not be "news" at all! Surprise your fiancée about your decision to take that job in Fish Haven, Idaho, and you may have some lovely evenings angling alone on Bear Lake.

It works the same in the business world. Many companies do a big business at what is called an industry trade show. There's a Hardware Show, an Electronics Show, a Gourmet Show, a Toy Fair, and so on. People come from all over the world to buy and sell goods in these categories. And if you are an exhibitor, you'd better not surprise your key accounts. Most national sales managers will "franchise in" any big customer about the whole program as a courtesy matter. You wouldn't want your top account standing there in the booth surprised at your new product or new pricing.

Understanding the role you play in the lives of other people will help keep you out of trouble, too. Learn to enjoy the differences in people and their expectations. Marketing types earn big bucks to do this. The payoffs for you will be even greater.

∽

BEING ADAPTABLE

Successful businesses are flexible, creative, and adaptable. You must learn to adopt new roles, adapt existing ones, and divest yourself of ones that no longer meet your interests.

Each business has a unique life span. For instance, the hula hoop life cycle was very short, while the yo-yo has been around over a hundred years. Every business operates on some kind of cycle that includes start-up, adolescence, adulthood, and a waning process.

Look at the Hudson Bay Company. More than three hundred years ago it was trading pelts. Had it allowed itself to dry up when the beaver skinning business matured and declined, "the Bay" would not be in existence today. It has had remarkable success in extending the life cycle of its striped blankets over the generations. Obviously, the businesses that started the company are quite different from the retail environment where the Bay operates today so successfully in Canada.

L. L. Bean runs a highly successful mail order catalog out of Freeport, Maine. It started with hunting boots in a "trading post" atmosphere and has totally taught itself how to excel in a multi-product national direct-order environment. The lessons learned in retailing and catalog marketing

> EVERY GOOD COMPANY HAS TO PREPARE FOR THE ABANDONMENT OF EVERYTHING IT DOES.
> —PETER DRUCKER

are quite different. The Bean organization has learned to survive and prosper in businesses no one ever imagined in 1910.

And so it must be with us. We have got to go on! Above all else, we must continue to relate to the real world of today and make provisions for the world of tomorrow. In so doing we learn to grow into new roles, whether it be a husband, a father, or a friend. By heeding examples of others and dealing with the changes, we can be successful in new roles.

Lawyers have long been calling the corporation a "legal person." By that they mean that the corporation lives on after the death or sale of any of its important components. As a person, you, too, must also learn to extend your useful life by adding, replacing, merging, and ending roles that are no longer appropriate. Refocusing your roles requires teaching old dogs new tricks. Sorry; there's no other way around it.

Clearly, the skills needed to crank up a business proposition are not the ones needed to grow or mature it. Think about what must take place for a business to clear all the hurdles leading to middle age. First there is a creative spark that must be kindled and coddled along. An enterprise is very tender at that stage. Then you must feed it the right resources to grow the right mix of talent and skills. If not, it won't meet the demands of its customers. About now, the business must learn to do something no other business can do as well; it must find a niche in the world so that its customer population will turn to it first. Then it must learn to deliver on its promises in an efficient manner. The cutthroats will beat it at its own game if it cannot adapt to stiff competitive pressures. For the first time, the business must actually shrink; it must cut the fat. Then the mature product, one with a distinct competitive advantage, can be delivered reliably to customers who have grown in sophistication.

These are all very different kinds of skills. The CEO may not be able to change his or her roles fast enough to be effective. In that case, the CEO can and should go off and relate to a new business idea, one whose needs match his or her skills. The CEO can then take the new enterprise to the point where he or she no longer enjoys the relationship.

In your personal life as well, some roles are temporary, so treat them as such. An entrepreneur can only conduct a business with the "one-person" philosophy for so long. A new enterprise needs nurturing and nearly maniacal direction, but soon, if it is successful, it outlives the need for a dictator. Professional management is needed, and the founder has a choice: learn to relate to the operation as a manager or lose it entirely. Parents need to understand this same principle as they struggle with their maturing children. They must learn to change and grow along with the young people—or else lose them. Anyone who has ever spent time at a family reunion knows how frustrating it is when relatives can't see how you've grown or changed and how that means relationships must change commensurately. Siblings, parents, aunts, and uncles have a funny way of following old patterns of behavior that have long outlived their usefulness. And us? What do we do? Well, more often than not, we fall into the old monkeyshines and fitfulness we displayed as adolescents. Anyone who doesn't believe in the power that roles exert on our behavior must also be a person who has avoided all family weddings.

Companies have these kinds of problems too—especially the ones with well-defined products. The aspiration of every marketer is to create a brand that is well known and recognizable, one that stands for something. Unless you're known for something, can be relied on to deliver something, or obviously stand for something, no one will notice what you have to offer. But it's a two-edged sword. If a market campaign is successful, the public may be unwilling to accept some other offer further down the road.

On the other hand, if customers need a business to come up with a new solution, the firm can't say, "Sorry, we're not creative." It can't say, "That's not our job." Yes, the company can decide to be in the business or out of it, but once involved, the customer relationship develops a life of its own that requires flexibility and creativity. By the same token, you cannot fail to act in a specific role simply because it pulls you into new worlds. Your commitment is to the relationship, not to a comfortable routine.

To play your unique roles more effectively, determine the needs of the particular relationships involved—your "audience." Upstart companies often hit on success when they find a new way to meet consumers' needs. The old supplier may have become married to activities that once worked in a certain marketplace—but the marketplace has changed, and consumers want something new. The newcomer doesn't radically change the rules, and it doesn't necessarily have a better product. It just does a better job of delivering the product that the customers have come to want. It acts in a more appropriate role posture.

Domino's Pizza is a great example. A few years back, it identified pizza customers' desires much better than the old pizza giants had. People want pizza delivered! They have for years. The old-line firms said delivery wasn't economical; they had dining rooms they needed to fill to cover their overhead. But pizza eaters don't care about those internal issues, and the organization that relates best to its external environment (rather than its own internal needs) successfully wins the prize. Today, Domino's is the largest deliverer of pizza in the world. It didn't reinvent the pizza; it simply found a new and better way to sell an old product.

Your life can demonstrate the same creative flexibility if you don't allow yourself to become trapped by the various personas you present to the world. *Persona* is a word from the Greek, meaning, "mask." Personas are a necessary and useful part of life; ideally, each "mask" should reflect the real you in some way. But if you find flexibility a problem, your personas may be getting in the way. For instance, as a doctor, you may identify so much with your white coat that you've lost your individuality.

Be careful. The argument we made earlier for meeting others' expectations has nothing to do with being a robot. Sometimes people get trapped in their roles. In effect, they live stereotypes. Growing in your roles—and sometimes growing out of them—is not a luxury. The job is easier if there is a model. Unfortunately, there is not always a model. Who knows how a DVD distributor ought to act? There have never been any before. However, if they act the way the DVD buyers expect them to act, they will be successful in that role.

You should seek out new ideas and behaviors that will contribute to your growth in a particular role. Very few parents learn their jobs from the signals sent by their children—if they have behavioral problem, they probably need more attention. Try spending more time with them. Experiment with behaviors you suspect may benefit you in new ways. If the experimentation makes you feel uncomfortable, that's all the more reason to persist. Those feelings are symptoms of successful growth.

Life is a stage. Play your roles well.

See if you can begin to understand your roles and how they relate to one another. The boss in you may or may not get along very well with the parent or spouse in you. By prioritizing and managing your roles, you can better react to other people's needs:

- *What roles do you play in your life?*

- *What are your objectives, methods, skills, and rewards for each role?*

- *Which role has the highest priority in your life?*

- *Where is each of these roles on the life-cycle curve?*

- *What expectations do other people have of you in each role?*

- *If you are in the process of making a significant life decision, how will each role react?*

- *How flexible, creative, and adaptable are you as you play these roles?*

Two

Do the right thing, and you'll do the right things

Ethical business is good business;
the honest person can succeed in any role.

H onesty is a real, concrete, and rare quality. We live in a culture of relativism, where people at every level of society convince themselves it's all right to tell lies in certain situations. Just about all of us have gone along with these untruths at one time or another, by commission or omission. Humankind in general has never been comfortable with the absolute truth-tellers in its midst.

But let's get this much straight: In both business and personal lives, the winners are always the ones who say what they will do and do what they will say. Long-term success is based on honest-to-goodness caring and a commitment to a message worth sending. You can have all the brains in the world, but without intellectual integrity, you're lost. As the following good business practices demonstrate, being real is always the best policy.

BEING YOURSELF

Successful businesses interact with customers in a variety of ways. You can interact differently in various relationships and still be yourself.

In order to be effective, you must communicate with people in the language they know. You have to base your pace on the local taste. And you are most effective when you are confident in who you are. When you are honest with yourself, you will be honest with others. Many people, however, think that acting in different ways with different people makes you a hypocrite. Nothing could be further from the truth. In fact, trusting yourself to act honestly in ways that are appropriate to the circumstance makes you more "real" than if you constantly and consistently tried to maintain some artificial model of yourself. You'll find that relating to each situation separately is very liberating. It is just the opposite of hypocrisy, for it frees you to express different facets of your personality with integrity. It's an amazing paradox.

We mentioned in the last chapter that one way to manage your roles is to understand others' expectations. But that doesn't mean you have to be a slave to those expectations. The idea isn't to become a social chameleon; you don't need to always act the way everybody wants. Decide the goals to which you wish to devote yourself, and then focus on developing mutually beneficial relationships with the people who can help you achieve those goals. Be yourself, truly yourself. Then get into situations that are natural for you. You'll probably learn that you do well in a variety of situations.

If you give yourself permission to be yourself, you'll enjoy yourself naturally and honestly. But remember, you don't serve everybody.

Most people have many roles, and these roles call for a wide range of behaviors. Ask any working mother. Her ability to amuse her toddler by squeaking like a mouse would be no more appropriate in a boardroom than her silk business suit would be at baby-bathing time. What's more, sooner or later, the working mother's separate roles will conflict. For instance, her toddler will come down with a fever on the same day her big presentation is due. The resolution of this inevitable conflict will not always be the same.

Unchanging, machine-like behaviors are not the way to avoid dishonesty. People can find upfront and highly creative ways to juggle conflicting roles. First, they have to be truthful with themselves about their skills, preferences, priorities, and limitations. It is important to know your core values and work from there. This information will help them determine how to fill both roles as best they can while accepting the inherent conflicts they adopted when they assumed these roles. It also means they have to be responsible for each of their actions; they can no longer hide behind some persona that may have outlived its usefulness. And this calls for honesty, with themselves and everyone else involved.

Businesses understand this. They don't view themselves as schizophrenic or hypocritical because they approach their markets in different ways. Look at the Clorox company, for example. It has built a sizable business by telling customers their laundry needs Clorox bleach. The active ingredient of this product is sodium hypochlorite, a powerful bleaching agent; the label warns you to be careful with it. Not far from Clorox on the supermarket shelf, the company presents another product called Clorox 2. Guess what? No chlorine. It says so right on the package, where it also says that Clorox 2 is safer for colored clothes than regular bleach. The company has been perfectly upfront about the differences in these two products. And some Clorox 2 customers would never consider buying original Clorox.

Does this make Clorox a hypocrite because its two products cause it to talk out of both sides of its corporate mouth? No way! People want clean clothes—and the Clorox company offers them different ways to get their clothes clean. The company has two market segments, and it's wise and proper to treat them differently.

If Clorox's leaders had defined the company as a chlorine-based liquid bleach outfit, the whole segment of people who want non-chlorine bleach would have been left out. The corporation wisely chose not to base its identity on a particular product. Instead, it opted to create a relationship with people who want clean clothes. Wherever that relationship leads, Clorox is going to take the trip—with a group of loyal customers who have a need the company can fill.

> IF WE BELIEVE IN UNLIMITED QUALITY, TREAT EACH OTHER WITH CARE AND RESPECT, AND ACT IN ALL OUR BUSINESS DEALINGS WITH TOTAL INTEGRITY, THE REST WILL TAKE CARE OF ITSELF.
>
> —FRANK PURDUE

In your own life, if you have only one way to behave, you're drastically and unnecessarily limiting the people with whom you can relate. You'll only stymie yourself if you permit a single "standard" response to every situation. Eventually, people will write you off. Meanwhile, you'll find that your toughest competitor, whether on the ball field or in the boardroom, is the one who can routinely draw from the widest array of techniques and approaches. These creative and adaptive competitors will learn your stock approaches to the situation, and they'll be able to preempt you routinely. As a result, you'll often be frustrated. You'll conclude that people don't appreciate you or what you have to say. And you'll be right.

The fact is that most of them didn't even hear you. You've become so fixed in your approach, thinking, and delivery that they don't need to wait to hear what you're going to say or do. They already know. Your commitment to a particular style has you frozen. If you were committed to relationships, however, that commitment would have kept you growing and learning. Instead, you've become obsolete.

The chess master has any number of moves that are solid winners. If you have only a few, you've lost before you've started, because the masters are out there, everywhere. The idea is to come up with enough variety in your game that the competition isn't sure what you'll try next.

That doesn't mean you have a license to be a nut. You need to be true to your core values. Customers expect a certain level of integrity every time. They want consistency, but they want it with a little spice now and then. I recall a radio station that had the concept down pat. They promoted themselves as offering "variety you can count on." The people in your life want the same thing.

Be you, but don't be dumb. Sit up straight and keep your elbows off the table when the boss comes to dinner. Wear a tie when you go to get a bank loan; you don't want to give the bank officers reasons to throw you out. Being appropriate does not mean being hypocritical. Your integrity is not defined by your dress, your manners, or your hairstyle.

By the same token, it's okay to give your mailman a different gift than you give the paperboy. And you better find something altogether different for your mother! Recognize that you have a variety of gifts; different people will like different things you have to offer. So connect with those people. Then just be yourself. As we said in chapter one, know your audience and use that knowledge to tailor the way you deliver your message. In other words, speak the same language as your listeners. Find their hot buttons so you can make your point. Then offer them the real you.

⤬

CREATING GOALS

A successful business has a plan that covers each of its ventures. In the same way, you should create goals that cover a variety of areas of your life.

To get what you want in life you need a plan. And if you're going to be honest, you need to be upfront about the fact that you're working a situation to fulfill your own goals. You have set out to win that promotion, achieve the best grades, or take the prettiest girl to the prom. You've developed a strategy, disciplined yourself to accomplish it, and are executing your plan.

The fact that you've plotted and orchestrated the whole affair, however, doesn't mean you're manipulative. It's all aboveboard. You're not aiming to achieve your goal by taking it away from anyone else, nor are you trying to change anyone to suit your purposes. You're going to succeed by making changes in your own actions, which in turn will encourage others, with their free will intact, to respond in ways that are mutually advantageous. That's a wonderful thing to do. Businesses do it every single day.

The idea is to establish a workable rapport with people. Discover commonalities and create empathy. Do it any way you can. Smile if they smile; frown if they frown. Again, you're not being a hypocrite; your goal is to get in step with them, not to become permanently like them. If you don't first build some kind of bridge between you, however, your chances of "selling them" are very slim. You need to create some kind of rapport; then you'll at least get a shot at the sale. Go find them wherever they are and establish a common rhythm; then, once you're in sync, you can shift gears and take them along with you.

Like the Clorox company, you may have one set of goals for a particular relationship and a different set for another. Don't allow those goals to become confused. If you're a lawyer, for example, success in the courtroom will not be defined in the same way you would define your goals for a particular friendship; friends seldom appreciate being lectured or interrogated. By the same token, if you're going for a job interview, you shouldn't grandstand about social issues, politics, or religion. Of course you have opinions on a wide range of topics, but discipline yourself to do what you're there to do, which in this case is to get the job. A job interview is not a debating society or a forum in which you are obligated to tell everything. Tell the truth and only the truth; don't hide anything; answer questions frankly—but be clear about your goals for that particular situation.

Also, be careful how you define success. For instance, if you're trying to secure a loan, success means getting that loan. But if you define success as getting the loan while wearing whatever clothes you want, you may be putting the core issue at risk. Is it worth taking that chance? Put on a tie, get the loan, buy the house . . . then put on your crazy clothes and throw a wild party with all your friends. Is this selling out? Absolutely not! Nobody loses. In fact, the mortgage company gets a swell new customer, and you and your

> A FOOLISH CONSISTENCY IS THE HOBGOBLIN OF LITTLE MINDS.
> —RALPH WALDO EMERSON

friends can have a ball Saturday night. Invite the loan officer and burn the tie. I'll bet he shows up in blue jeans.

When you have a goal in mind, you also have to be willing to try as many approaches as necessary until you succeed. The focus should be on accomplishment, not on maintaining a consistent method. Be willing to reevaluate the means you use to achieve your plans. Rethink your strategies. Don't worry what people will think if you change your tactics, and don't let your pride in your own position make you rigid. Be true to the deepest, realest you. Your commitment is to your goal, not to a particular method.

Have that goal clear in your mind before you step out onto the various stages of your life. Know your lines ahead of time. Strategizing the best way to express yourself is not deceptive. This approach simply means you exert the discipline necessary to think through something in advance. Stick to your game plan and then trust yourself.

❧

HAVING INTEGRITY

Successful businesses lead the market rather than follow it. Likewise, you should let your inner self shape your outer roles.

Expressing your true self in a variety of ways is very different from needing the approval of everyone you meet. People who are desperate to make a good impression may lose touch with who they really are. They forget their true values. Pretending to be something you're not only complicates your life. In the end, it erodes your composure and self-confidence.

Be aware of which people have significant roles to play in your goals for a particular situation. You don't need to form a connection with *everybody*. For instance, at that job interview we mentioned earlier, don't go in and brown-nose every clown in the office, from the receptionist to Mr. Big. The idea isn't to burst in and gush all over every person you pass. Instead, reach out to the people who approach you in the context of the interview; compliment them on the things you'd comment on if you didn't need the job. Be genuine. And if by chance you receive a compliment in return, and it's deserved, simply say "thank you." Know your own strengths, and don't be afraid to express your knowledge. That's a different kind of honesty; it's called self-awareness, and it can actually be a form of humility. The truly humble person knows not only her limitations but her strengths as well. That's real integrity.

Furthermore, cooperation with people with whom you don't agree doesn't mean you've sold out. You don't have to agree with a person on *everything* to cooperate with him on *something*. Life isn't an all-or-nothing affair. Some roles dovetail with others. Some do not. You have to be sophisticated about it. Keep your moral standards, but don't confuse moral and tactical issues. Learn from the example of some people who walked this thin line:

- Jesus ate with the tax collectors and talked with the prostitutes.

- Churchill and Roosevelt made a pact with the villain—Stalin—in order to defeat another monster—Hitler.

- Alexander Hamilton and James Madison had fundamentally different ideas about how a new nation should be governed—but they worked together to ratify the U.S. Constitution.

Katherine Graham, the late publisher of the *Washington Post*, stands as the quintessential example of role sophistication for her handling of the Vietnam-era Pentagon Papers. She pursued her organization's self-interest without compromising her integrity. She could attend a press luncheon with Richard Nixon while instructing her editors to publish the secret papers in defiance of Nixon's administration. She acted in the public interest as she saw it, fulfilling her most fundamental responsibility as a publisher. And yet she maintained her dignity, propriety, charm, and integrity while doing so. While she made sure her facts were straight and told the truth, she let the chips fall where they would. Hers was a sacred trust, and she carried it out, in business and in life, with class.

We can be that way, too.

Knowing who you are and what you're after is one of the keys to success. It turns out to be one of the toughest ethical issues, too. If you're not sure what you want, you'll easily be swayed into doing things that turn out to be less than desirable. You'll waste a lot of people's time, including your own. You'll make commitments that you'll carry out only half-heartedly.

The business world confronts this challenge all the time. The marketplace constantly pulls companies in all sorts of directions—that's why companies have business strategies. These already-formulated plans remind them of why they exist and how they should react to emerging market conditions. Believe it or not, profit alone is not the determining factor for most companies. A particular product may make money in the short run—but in the long run, producing and marketing that product may damage the integrity of the entire company. Oddly enough, a capitalist business firm sometimes has to say "no" to production opportunities.

If a business said "yes" to even a fraction of the opportunities it could legally and easily pursue, the company and its managers would go nuts. They'd be all over the place. And with their focus and resources so scattered, they would endanger their organizational energy. This doesn't mean that a company can't pursue a variety of ventures. But much soul-searching goes on within the company so that it's ready when opportunity knocks . . . ready to say "yes" but just as important, self-aware enough to say "no." And believe me, that takes guts.

At both the corporate and personal levels, the greatest dishonesty isn't even intentional. It is sad to see people, of any age, focus on some stereotypical view of who they should be. It is being dishonest with yourself to pursue a particular college degree, for instance, just because your parents, girlfriend, or teacher thinks you should. It's a misfortune that occurs when we focus so much on some outside definition of what we want that we lose touch with what's really going on inside us. This is a tremendously wasteful circumstance. For a business it could cost billions of dollars. As an individual you could lose not only time and money but something much more valuable—yourself. You could end up living a lie.

Figure out what you want, and then don't allow people to swerve you from your goals. There will always be people who will try to push you in other directions, but don't allow yourself to be shaped by their desires. They may love you; you may ache to have them love you, but do not give them the wheel. If necessary, simply tell them to go away. Be committed to your true self and make that commitment your highest priority.

⚓

Delivering on Your Promises

Businesses and individuals are defined by their relationships and how they "deliver." You should have integrity in your relationships, delivering on your promises.

Integrity is at the heart of good business. A record of good business ethics goes right to the bottom line; it gives you a considerable competitive advantage. Being really you and really believing in what you're doing pays dividends because it allows you to form enduring relationships based on trust.

A certain value is created by a relationship. In a business, the enterprise will be defined more by what the customer gets out of it than by what the seller puts into it. Value is established, whether in a business or in our personal lives, not by what we think we're doing but by what others achieve as a result of our actions. The corollary is that we cannot possibly succeed either in business or in our personal lives unless our idea of what delivers a benefit ties very closely to what the other person perceives as valuable.

One of the silliest things I've seen, both in corporate life and personal endeavors, is when people go off into an ivory tower or some other form of seclusion to try to find the next greatest trend, or "themselves." If we really understand that it's our relationships that define us, then we realize such hermit behavior can only reduce our understanding of the world. It limits our ability to find our unique place in the world's relationships, and thus it gets us no closer to finding our real selves.

What you're looking for, more than anything else is a match that works. This is true whether in a personal relationship or a business endeavor. To find a productive match, you need to understand yourself well enough to know what you will and will not do. A person who knows what he or she can and cannot do will better serve the customers' needs than someone who doesn't. In your personal life as well, knowing the people you're dealing with can enhance your match. Know their needs and make every attempt within your parameters to fill them.

Be slow and cautious when you commit to anything, whether it's a new business venture or a new relationship. There are always risks associated with saying "yes". Make sure you promise only what you can deliver and deliver at least what you promise. Once you've made a commitment, however, be wholly dedicated. Your reputation is on the line every day. If you fail to live up to your word even once, how are you going to convince anyone to believe you the next time?

One of the major advantages of establishing trusting relationships is that, once they are in place you don't have to work so hard every day to fill your needs. The harmony generated in a stable relationship has great value—efficiency. You can get on with business instead of dickering over ground rules, reworking sour deals, or covering your steps. When you are in a trusting relationship—business or personal—you know where each other is coming from and what to expect.

Business as a whole has trouble convincing the public that it operates ethically because buffoons and shortsighted sharkies will always hog the headlines. The reality, however, is that a crook makes only one sale, and he pays for his dishonesty with his future. Any legitimate businessperson knows that service is what makes business work, not charlatanry. Despite popularly held wisdom to the contrary, the world does not produce enough fools to keep the crooks in business. Yes, there are snake-oil salesmen. There are even, at any moment, *a lot* of snake-oil salesmen. But this book is about what we can learn from successful businesses, the ones that continuously turn a profit, while at the same time endowing their communities with funds for the arts or for the needy. A firm like this operates with consummate integrity—and makes a profit by doing so. Consumers know what it stands for, and they trade their hard-earned dollars for that consistent integrity. Real profit relies not on today's quick deal but on tomorrow's repeat business.

Ethical behavior pays. And the reason it pays is that people choose to repeatedly interact with the firms—or people—who will give them a fair deal. Act with gusto in every role you fill, throw your heart into whatever you do—and be ethical. If you do that repeatedly, the world will in return, cooperate with you repeatedly. People will choose to interact with you if they know they'll get a fair shake. Others will want to work with you because you create an atmosphere in which they can live upright lives. Still others will seek you out or volunteer to help you with no strings attached because they know you'll do right by them. People will choose to initiate and foster relationships with you.

DEVELOPING VALUED RELATIONSHIPS

Successful businesses increase the value or service to favored customers. You should give more to develop the most valued relationships.

The goal of most salespeople is to conduct their affairs in such a way that they help customers buy. There are three common mistakes that trip up their efforts. Number one, they may skip the "courtship" before the "wedding." They are too interested in the close. On the other hand, they may be so nervous about the act of closing that they pussyfoot around, failing to go for it. The third, and maybe greatest transgression is getting the first two right but then neglecting the customer. A business that neglects the customer is like the married man who ignores his wife and is then surprised when she walks out on him. The relationship doesn't end with the wedding.

Listen to the protocol associated with any sale: as the cash register rings its hallelujah over the transaction, the salesperson will say to the buyer, "Thank you." The salesperson indicates that the establishment appreciates what the customer has done. This translates into the perception that a debt has been created. As customers, we make the unspoken assumption that the seller owes us something. This means the next time we enter into a relationship with the seller, we are even more demanding. We expect more as the relationship grows. Many business relationships dissolve because the partners are not willing to give what is expected. Many divorces occur because of this as well.

Whether in business or your personal life, both parties of the relationship expect long-term value. (Obviously, it's best if both receive short-term value as well from every transaction. That's not always going to be the case, but it's certainly a worthwhile objective.) The proverbial snake oil salesman ignored the long term to his peril and was pretty much run out of town. Unless a buyer conducts several transactions with you, he is not really a customer. He is just a shopper. Relationships are what make customers loyal to a particular company. It's the same with people. You need to make it easy and pleasant for people to come back to you, as a business or as an individual.

Remember, repeat business requires that you maintain your credibility; you do what you say and say what you'll do. Be honest with people about what you can do for them and what you can't. Some of the strongest relationships I have in the business world are with people who have told me they couldn't help but knew of someone who could. The same is true with personal relationships. Let people know your boundaries. That way they won't expect something you can't deliver.

If you can, however, in both personal relationships and in business dealings, try to anticipate what the other side in the relationship is going to need; then have a solution ready for them before they even realize they are going to want it. The specific solution is not as important as the confidence you are building.

Make it easy and worthwhile for people to deal with you. Don't let the peculiarities of your

> "I AM THE WORLD'S WORST SALESMAN; THEREFORE, I MUST MAKE IT EASY TO BUY."
> —F. W. WOOLWORTH

personality get in the way. Simplify the interactions. Give people what you promise, and seek the mutual benefit. You've got to find needs you want to fill and can feel good about satisfying. Put value within convenient reach for both sides of the relationship, so the cycle can be effortlessly repeated. Take ongoing responsibility for your relationships—or they may disappear.

Everyone makes mistakes of course. Sometimes, when you can't fix the goof-up, fix the relationship instead. Luckily, as loyalty is hard to create, it is also hard to lose. The customer is an asset far more valuable than any you can find on a balance sheet. And in our personal lives, securing and maintaining good relationships is what makes life worth living.

⤲

ADAPTING TO GROWING RELATIONSHIPS

Enduring businesses adapt themselves to the obligations of their market roles. You, too, should bend, curve, and grow within the context of your relationships.

Being true to yourself is important. Few of us, however, are free spirits who can express ourselves in whatever way our fancy moves. Sometimes, because we are already committed to certain relationships, we must accept the obligations that come with the turf. This means we may have to work out compromises with the significant others in our lives—but it doesn't mean we have to lose our own integrity.

An example from nature, the bristlecone pine, gives us a good idea how we can mold ourselves to the environment while remaining distinctly ourselves. Those bristlecones are some of the longest-lived plants in the world. They've been molded and contorted every which way for millennia. But they've survived because they accommodate a situation without surrendering any of their basic essence. They're uniquely successful at adapting to their environment while holding on to their identity. No one who has ever climbed the White Mountains of California to see the bristlecone pine forest would ever say that these majestic beauties were not craggily and clearly unique.

One of humankind's most painful errors is expressed by the oft-repeated lament, "If only they would change." In general, the people around us *aren't* going to change, not ever. And if by chance they do, they will do so because *they* have decided to change—not because we have needed them to do so. Once we recognize that fact, we can take responsibility for our own lives. The appropriate question then becomes: "What can I do, right now, to change my *actions* to improve this situation?" Notice the question is not "How can I change *myself*?" Adapting to the demands of a particular relationship doesn't mean I force myself to become something I'm not. Instead, the issue is: "What can I do with the self I have to move things along? How can I present myself in a different way that will help me achieve my goals for this relationship?" In some cases, where you've tried everything without success, you may need to ask: "Where can I find the people who want what it is I have to offer?"

Adapt yourself to the demands of a particular role. Be flexible; find new and creative ways to express the real you. Remember, the concept of role sophistication is rooted firmly in truth to yourself and others. There is no other way for it to work. Your big payoffs in life will come only through a consistent policy of personal integrity. Develop in yourself a subtle but pervasive quality of industrious ethics. Work to personify the "ethical alternative" in the crowd. Your relationships—both business and personal—will benefit as a result.

I know, I know: ever since you were a child people have been telling you that honesty is good. It's how good people behave; it's the moral choice. All that may be true—but I'm telling you that honesty is also the *smartest* option. Being honest is the most efficient way to operate. The truth requires the least energy to explain and maintain. It allows people to choose to interact with you time and time again. And these repeated choices cause efficiency, which drives profit. Role sophistication combined with integrity makes for the only workable human alternative.

The best, most profitable companies in the world operate on these principles. Remaining truly themselves, they tailor-make solutions that genuinely serve human needs. They also specifically say "no" to activities outside the realm of their expertise and mission. They stand for something, make commitments to markets, and back up what they say. Our best relationships already work this way. You need only to apply these techniques to a broader range of situations, opportunities, and acquaintances.

That's how businesses stay in the black. And that's how you can stay in the pink.

Select one of the most honest people and one of the least honest people you know. As best you can, consider the lives and behaviors of these individuals in light of the business practices discussed in chapter two:

- *Do these individuals say what they do and do what they say?*
- *Are they honest with themselves as well as other people?*
- *Do they have strategies that include all their ventures?*
- *How are these individuals defined by their relationships?*
- *Do they protect their relationships? If so, how?*
- *Do their relationships grow deeper, stronger, and more valuable with time?*
- *How do these individuals adapt themselves to the various contexts of their lives?*

How can you better portray ethical qualities in your own life? How can you avoid dishonesty and hypocrisy?

Three

FIND YOUR PURPOSE, AND YOU'LL FIND YOUR PAYOFFS

Sell what your "customers" need and want;
maximize the value of each role in your life.

Businesses prosper when they set out to understand people and then make the sacrifices necessary to develop things for which people are willing to pay. The better companies overcome their own second thoughts and internal conflicts by focusing their resources on serving customers. As paradoxical as it may seem, getting what we want results from getting others what they want. The rewards of happiness and prosperity can't be attained directly; we must earn them by marshaling our talents and resources toward *serving a purpose*. Be sure you're good at something you like and that something you do well solves other people's problems. Life's payoffs are earned by getting outside of ourselves to deliver what others value.

> IF YOU WANT A FULL HOUSE, YOU GIVE THE PUBLIC WHAT IT WANTS.
> —BERT LAHR

HELPING OTHERS

Businesses exist and continue to survive by serving needs. Your personal life will thrive as well when you meet the needs of those around you.

No company stays long in operation if it fails to contribute to the comfort, convenience, or progress of its customers. The ones that do this well, and support their products and services with after-the-sale attention, tend to grow. Those that fail to serve, and to serve well, fail.

If a firm becomes more interested in its own welfare than it is in ministering to the needs of the people who contributed to its success, the customer population will cut that firm off at the knees. Customers are ruthless. They're unforgiving, and they should be.

As an individual, you can learn a lesson from this interaction between corporation and customer. You, too, have constituencies that need and want what you have to offer. Discipline yourself to develop the talents and passions that will make your "output" valuable to others. Get outside of yourself to determine what it is that you can do to help others. When you do, others will reward you for your efforts. You have to take the leap of faith that they will do so. It is the same risk every business confronts as it lays its offer on the table every day.

I can see you wincing at the analogy; thinking of business as a public service is hard for most people. Most people think corporations can run roughshod over the public and still continue to prosper. It may look that way sometimes, but such behavior always catches up with an organization. P. T. Barnum may have been right—a sucker may actually be born every minute—but latter-day Barnums throughout the corporate world have learned the hard way that suckers tend not to stay fooled for long. When they learn they were duped, they generally refuse to be suckered again.

And the same rules apply to human relations. You don't get ahead by stepping on others. No one has ever achieved long-term success by selling a shoddy product or failing to deliver what was promised. You succeed by developing what others want and delivering what they expect. Create something of physical value, or some irreplaceable service; that makes you someone's prime choice when it comes time to serve his or her need.

Think of it as your effort to turn a well-earned profit, interpersonally. You want the other parties in your life to derive immense satisfaction both from "the deal" and the relationship it engenders. They'll send you "business"—and come back for more themselves. Just remember that life's payoffs don't come when you aim for those rewards as your top priority, through whatever shortcuts you can find. The payoffs are byproducts of your real goal: serving others.

If corporations want more profit, they figure out what their customers really like about what they do—and they do more of it. If you want to increase your income, find out what your employer really pays you to do—and give it the gas. If you want to increase your emotional income from a personal relationship, act and speak in the ways that make people want to deal with you. Don't complain. And don't look down your nose at the idea of service. If you think serving others is the domain of the downtrodden, maybe you should drive around and see where some of these "servants" live in your community; after all, doctors and lawyers are both service providers.

No owner-operator of an ongoing business is successful at what he does without doing far more for others than he set out originally to do for himself. It's a curious twist that even the most crass, money-hungry proprietors will, over the long haul, find ways of modifying their selfishness to achieve their desired results. Often that means, strangely enough, acting in the most fair and even generous way toward others.

Alfred Adler, early in the twentieth century, formulated the same principle. He challenged depressed persons to venture out daily to do something significant for someone else. Doing so would relieve their dejection within a week, he said. Adler's advice has been borne out in popular wisdom ever since. In order to help others, a person must first ignore her own problems, escape from entrenched patterns of thinking, and dedicate herself to the creative process of understanding someone else—to the point of discovering whatever it is that would please the other person. In going outside of the self to create and serve, we can get our own acts together even more.

There is a sad, deep, and totally unnecessary void in the world's ability to satisfy aching human needs. Those who try hard enough to close the gap generate an investment return that is the envy of venture capitalists everywhere.

<hr>

Focusing Your Energies

Successful businesses commit themselves to supplying specific products to specific markets. In a similar way, choose what you will be and focus your energies on growing in that role.

When I was a little boy, my neighborhood church had a service at seven-thirty on Sunday evenings. No other church in our town had such a time slot. "Why?" I asked the priest. He told me: "Raymond, there are lots of people in the city who travel, who work strange hours, who may have family in the hospital, or who for any number of reasons are not able to get to church on Sunday morning. We don't want to close the door on them." This pastor was doing three unique things: First, he organized around customers' needs, not his own—even if that meant missing his favorite TV show: *Bonanza*. Second, he identified a target market outside his local territory; he was serving a citywide audience of worshippers with certain needs. Third, he was ministering to people who really wanted the service he had to offer.

Most individuals do a very mediocre job of life. They take the easy way out, doing only what is expected rather than focusing their energies on seeking and targeting specific needs. But if you follow the approach of my neighborhood priest, you'll find a greater pay-off. At least some people get exactly what they want. If you go out of your way to detect and solve problems no one else wants or knows how to fix, the entire world may not beat a path to your door—but some people certainly will.

One of the more pernicious myths afoot in modern society is that closing the door on an opportunity will rob a person of happiness. Don't close any options off for yourself. Stay ready for anything. Well, it is exactly that kind of thinking that keeps so many companies drifting from crisis to crisis—and too many people roaming aimlessly, waiting for the big thing to hit. The fact is, unless you are a very, very lucky human being, you have a slim chance of striking it rich by waiting for the entire garden of opportunity to burst into bloom. You'd do better to focus your fertilizer and pruning on a few specific plants.

In other words, you have to walk through door A or door B or door C—one, but not all three. Unless you open one of those gift doors, you will have nothing. Yes, it's true: The moment you say "yes" to a particular goal, you more or less say "no" to other opportunities. And yes, someday, one of those missed opportunities may strike you as something you should have pursued. But, believe me, those wistful feelings won't hurt nearly as badly as the long-term consequences of refusing to commit to anything. You have to cast your lot with someone or something.

I know of a large firm whose owner was actually reluctant to engage in corporate planning because he was concerned that the moment a plan identified particular business opportunities, the entire staff would fail to recognize other commercial enterprises that could bring a high return on investment. By the same token, I know a lot of guys who are still running around in their mid-thirties because they don't want to commit to one woman; their lives look sadly unsatisfying to me.

Take a look at your own life. If you're afraid of being over-committed, you may keep your schedule so open that you commit to nothing—you'll end up accomplishing very little. Or you may go to the opposite extreme: you feel obliged to serve on every possible committee or volunteer for any good cause that comes along. As a result, you're pulled in so many different directions that you have little energy to do anything well. You would do better to determine what you do best, and then focus your time and effort on those opportunities that most enhance your personal skills while helping the world. Look at every decision, every choice you have, as an opportunity to gain some control over who you are as a person and what your future might be. Learn when to say "no"—and when to say "yes."

Many companies make investment choices based on fears that they will be left out of a particular market segment that could be hot a few years from now. This happens in part because corporate chieftains worry about being overly dependent on any one particular marketplace of the business they have chosen. Diversification—getting into many different lines of business—can be a good thing, but not up to the point that it

> THERE ARE MANY THINGS IN LIFE THAT WILL CATCH YOUR EYE, BUT ONLY A FEW WILL CATCH YOUR HEART. PURSUE THESE.
> —MICHAEL NOLAN

spreads a company too thin and impairs its ability to act quickly on any front. These companies may figure if they get into many different markets, whichever one turns out to be the hot one can be the locus of future investment. But think about it for a moment: If a firm is stretched thin with financial commitments to many different business units, it won't have the cash available to throw into the new, hot business of the moment—presuming such a dream business can be identified before everyone else has already gotten into it.

You want to be like a crescent wrench. This tool really has only one purpose. It's not a hammer. It's not even very effective as an all-purpose wrench. It exists to tighten or loosen nuts, bolts, and other hexagonal-headed hardware. But guess what? Within its "field of expertise," it is responsive to a wide range of different conditions. It is an effective and focused tool that can expand and contract in response to whatever size hardware you are trying to tighten or loosen. It adapts itself to the situation at hand but has one basic purpose.

And that is what you need to do. Pick what you will be, and then adapt to emerging needs in that area. If you are an aspiring author committed to writing your first novel in your spare time, then you may need to say *no* to weekend opportunities for partying. If parenting is one of your major purposes in life, you may need to let go of some volunteer activities. Life offers us many doorways. Just because a particular door exists, however, doesn't mean you have to walk through it. Choose carefully which doors you will open. Say *yes* only to those opportunities that will focus your specific skills to meet specific needs in the world around you.

～

Accepting Others' Needs

Successful companies do not try to change the needs of the people who depend on them. Likewise, you should accept and understand the actual needs of the important people in your life.

Most people constantly try to "improve" the people in their lives. "Why do you want that?" we say to them. "That doesn't make sense. Don't you know you'd be better off wanting such-and-such instead?" Many a human spends a lifetime telling those nearest and dearest to them just what it is they ought to want. Companies, on the other hand, do whatever they can to find out what the customer wants, and then they do their best to supply it. In this instance, people and companies spend their life energies on significantly different efforts. But the companies' approach is more productive, satisfying, and dramatically more likely to cause success.

Sure, a business may try to help someone change into what she dreams of being. The coffers of Revlon, *Esquire,* and Dexatrim would be bone-dry otherwise. But successful marketers don't go out and try to change society. They just tap into whatever people want to do anyway, and they offer their products to facilitate the realization of the buyers' dreams.

Not even the cleverest advertising minds can make people change. What top marketers try to do instead is find the need—say, to stop smoking—and then reach those needs on their own terms. The packaging, the copy, the tangible product, all the elements of contact seek to relate to that anxious individual on the verge of kicking the habit. And each of us must do that as well when targeting the emerging needs of those around us.

Trying to change people is the biggest waste of time. If you tell someone she's wrong, that person will feel more firmly than ever that she is right. Then you will have trouble relating to her in the future. She'll think you are a jerk. Take that same person, and spend time trying to discover her objectives. What does she want that she's not getting? Come up with a way to help her get it. Convince her you can understand where she wants to go, and then let her know your service or product will help her get there. Change will take care of itself; you will just be a convenient vehicle for the process. But guess what? She'll love you, and she'll remember you, and her happy memories will cause her to think of you again and again. Next time you have an offer, she will be back, and remember from the previous discussion: repeat business is what brings the payoffs.

Sometimes a business that lacks imagination and understanding will introduce a product just because it will utilize some production facility, or the research and development (R&D) pool, or whatever. The best companies, however, have learned a long time ago that this is self-defeating behavior. Why? Because the customers don't get anything out of it. The financial value that these schemes purport to deliver is always easy to prove on paper. The numbers people love them because such projects are alleged to use assets that are already in place more productively. But come on, it's clear that the only valid reason to introduce a new product is that the market wants it.

Some people, likewise, have a need to dispense advice. This is interesting, but it has nothing to do with the needs of your marketplace. Do not play out your internal needs in the marketplace. Unless you are very close to someone, or are responsible for his behavior, the time to give advice is when someone makes it clear that your input would be useful.

Customers don't care that the chairman's wife thought of some initiative or that manufacturing can get more efficient production runs with it or that the acquisition experts from headquarters will have numbers to fumble. Those are all internal factors. And when companies make moves in the marketplace that are really just disguised gifts to themselves, they better learn to enjoy them quickly. These are not the kind of gifts that keep on giving.

This is easy to see in people. Ever get a gift from someone who had a need for you to have this prize? Such gifts usually end up at the returns department. Give people gifts they want, especially ones they wouldn't buy for themselves. That's how you fill a need.

Finding the real need is very tricky business, for companies and individuals alike. Years ago, a singularly bright executive at Black & Decker summed up the problem very well: "People don't want quarter-inch drill bits. They want quarter-inch holes." You don't try to sell bits when people want holes. Sell them solutions to the hole-making problems.

Whatever you're selling—and any effort to win over other people is a sales effort—you must sell at the rate the market is buying.

Understand that others will place a value on what you produce, and that it's not always a rational value. You can influence the price they are willing to pay, but ultimately you have to accept the "going rate."

Value is determined not by what we "put in," but by what others "get out." Nobody really cares how much work or effort goes into the creation or delivery of anything. They just want what they can secure in the way of solutions to their problems and satisfaction of their needs. For instance, you may feel you are contributing enormously to your family by working long hours to bring home a sizeable income. But another family member may place little value on the particular service you are providing; instead, he would value more your presence and attention at family outings.

Deliver what customers value. Companies have to understand this in spades. Pizza Hut misunderstood to its peril, allowing Domino's to take over a huge slice of the pre-baked pizza business. Customers considered quick delivery as important a variable as taste and price. Pizza Hut was unduly influenced by the corporate number boys who wanted to see their prime asset (dining rooms) better utilized. The result? Pizza Hut kept promoting its restaurant dinners and redesigning its décor. It tried to revamp its retail appearance and get more "with it." And people liked the new trappings, but management missed the point. The buyers still preferred their old overstuffed chairs at home over the Pizza Hut redesign. Domino's picked up the slack by "delivering" what people really wanted: to stay home and enjoy an inexpensive, reliable meal. The people "bought" the Domino's idea. These customers did not care about issues such as dining room utilization no matter how many times they were redesigned.

When I got a haircut today, only one variable was important to me: Did the barber take the American Express card? I had not left home without it, and no other variable struck me as important. When you are an almost bald man, the AMEX sign in the barber's window is just about the most critical piece of information you need. I am sure that fact would be disappointing or even disturbing to the stylist who spent years learning her craft or to her bosses who just invested in their facility's decor, but it is, nonetheless, true. I want a no-frills barber who will take my American Express card. And luckily, today I found a barber who gave me what I wanted.

Companies are tremendously committed to figuring out what variables people will pay them to deliver. Individuals seldom demonstrate the same commitment. But we should.

You see, people, whether they are acting as consumers or purchasing vice presidents, do not make their product or idea selections based on any rational model. Do not believe them when they protest this assertion. They will not tell you the truth—mostly because they don't know the truth.

An alien landing at a grocery checkout line may be able to discern that a guy is buying film, candles, and chocolate chip cookies. What the customer has just exchanged his hard-earned money to buy, however, are things the alien can't grasp: memories, a romantic dinner, and a good time in the park with a toddler. A successful company understands its product's psychological aura—and it markets its product to meet the subtle emotional needs of its customers.

Sometimes that means infusing a tangible product like soap powder with an ethereal benefit like "springtime." Other times it means you don't try to sell perfume to folks, when they really want status. Instead, you make status even more glamorous and say how this perfume will reinforce it. You don't try to sell people on the income your bank's trust department can create for their estate, if the people want only security for what they've got today. You don't try to teach people, when all they want is someone to listen. And don't take the kids to the ballpark when all they want is to talk with you.

Address the motivation behind the need. That's the stuff from which satisfaction is made. Realize that what most people say they need is rarely their true concern. You've got to be able to really hear behind what people are saying. Don't make it up. Don't think for them. Don't put yourself in their place. What you'd be thinking in their shoes is totally irrelevant and probably counterproductive to any effort to understand their point of view. Commit to listening intently on a deeper level. It's a technique that works magic.

We all want an excuse to do what we are already inclined to do. A purchasing agent may pay a premium for delivery just to be sure that the materials reach the receiving department in time. Although pages of analysis will argue that companies make purchasing decisions based on very rational factors, do not be fooled. Long after all the product features are studied and compared, the biggest and brightest companies in America still trot out the "soft factors": reputation; the likelihood that the vendor will be in business in five years; how easy it was to work with you; or how charming, creative, or clever your salesperson was. Here, gut feel is masquerading as logic. It goes on every day in boardrooms the world over. It's also going on in kitchens and bedrooms the world over. And we should understand its dynamics.

Our job is to do everything we can to help both sides of our relationships achieve what they perceive as value. That way each party will want to rely on each other again and again. This is a highly efficient way of behaving, because this is how you avoid repeated "start-up" costs with new relationships. This is where the smart payoffs are.

〜⋙〜

BEING HONEST

Successful companies offer those services and products that are in their best interest. You, too, need to be upfront about what you have to offer in any given relationship.

Individuals routinely ask for raises because they just had a new baby and need the extra income. No effective boss has ever granted such a request. Raises happen because it's in the company's best interest to give them.

Understanding this phenomenon is one of the most important things that individuals can learn from businesses. Own what it is you have to sell. Help others see the value in what you bring to the party. Don't push the items. Explain the good things that happen to the one who buys what you have to offer. But don't make an offer that will cost you more than you can deliver.

You've also got to accept that you can't fill every one of your customer's needs. In fact, you've got to accept that you'll be able to fill only a very few. In looking for the right challenge to master, certain thresholds must be crossed:

- Is this opportunity consistent with the goals I've set for myself?

- Is the payoff worth it?

- Are the risks ones I can live with?

- Over the long stretch, is this a market I'd want to serve?

You can't do everything, nor should you. For instance, if a charity has asked you to volunteer your services and you want to oblige, you'd do well to offer the skills you genuinely possess; if you're a "numbers person" but terrible at social interactions, you'll probably do better offering to help with the charity's income tax forms rather than trying to counsel disturbed teenagers.

Better companies understand that their continued success is contingent upon an ongoing and concerted effort to deepen their understanding of themselves and their customers. When you decide on something, get in there and play as hard and as smart as you possibly can. That means developing even deeper commitments to what you can and won't do for customers. The proper posture is not to become so servile and obsequious with customers—or the important people in your life—that they run you ragged. I have no quarrel with the archetypal cleaning lady who announces before she is hired, "I don't do windows." She's defined the parameters of her service. It is up to you to decide if you want to contract with her or not.

Just because a customer asks for it, must you deliver? No. You can make two arguments:

- We don't do that because we couldn't do it as well or at the value that XYZ Company could do it. Here is their number.

- Even if we did do that, it would take away from our ability to do A, B, or C. Knowing what we do and sticking to it keeps us from doing a less than adequate job, because we accept only tasks at which we are organized to excel. We do want to serve. The way we serve is by doing these certain things (A, B, C) better than anyone else. (Then refer to No. 1 above.)

Serve a purpose and let people know what you stand for. Be careful about standing for too many things, or you'll confuse them (and yourself). Many of the better companies create new divisions when they want to come out with a product line that may dilute the image of the original company. They don't branch out like this until they're sure they have the resources to support their new ventures. You, too, can exercise the same wisdom. Your boss may be angry when he hears "that's not my job," but in some discreet, respectful way, you may need to get that point across. (And then you'd better shine at your job.)

❧

TAKING RESPONSIBILITY

Successful businesses take responsibility for initiating the interactions that lead to the payoffs. You, too, need to take the initiative to improve the relationships in your life.

Businesses exist to serve people efficiently. But they don't expect customers to spontaneously seek them out. Instead, they find a customer, give her something she wants but can't easily get, and in return expect that the customer will give them what they want—a profit, a payoff all at the company's initiative.

It's the same with people. We need to take responsibility for taking care of ourselves. We can't expect people to automatically come knocking on our doors, offering the relationships that will make our lives productive and valuable. We've got to act first. We begin the process by stretching to improve our capacity and dedication to find and fill others' needs.

Business firms do the homework that enables them to get their customers into the new world the customer already envisions. If a firm can articulate the buyer's problem for him, rapport is established. With rapport comes a chance to make a sale. The task for the enterprise, or for us, is to seek out and establish relationships outside ourselves.

Realize that people don't always know what they want, even though they can identify very specific details. People don't know what kind of vehicle they want, but it's blue. They don't know how many bedrooms their next house will have, but they are certain that they will have brass doorknobs. They're not sure what they expect from a spouse, but they know they want to feel important . . . or loved . . . or safe. This phenomenon is much more common than you may imagine. Don't expect the people in your life to define the exact behaviors they want from you. Instead, help them articulate what they want. Have a solution ready. Look for a challenge that inspires you.

To be successful, a business must anticipate the market's needs and its movements and prepare programs or products to meet them. Similarly, by anticipating the needs of your boss, you'll get her where she's trying to go. Devise and complete a project for her before she asks. Foresee the stresses your child will face in his new school—spend time now (rather than later) creating techniques and solutions that will help him cope. Don't wait for people to bring their problems to you. Focus on being proactive rather than reactive.

Understand that customers—and the people in your life—are not going to create a quantum-leap product for you. They may suggest minor, incremental improvements to what already exists, but they probably won't envision a brand-new product or service. Oddly enough, giving the customer exactly what she wants reduces innovation, because the average person says she already has everything she needs. The only way out of that box is to create something consistent with what you know about that person and then ask her, "Now, what do you think?" So take time first to listen; that way you'll understand what's truly needed. And then put on your thinking cap and come up with a breakthrough.

If you were a railroad owner in the 1920s, you could have polled your customers for suggested improvements. They might have told you your cars needed thicker window shades or softer seat covers. They would not have warned you about the airplane's potential invasion of your market. You'd have to understand their need for a smoother, quicker ride and act on that.

And so it is with people. Your girlfriend may be able to tell you to brush your teeth more often. It may be up to you to realize that you need your wisdom teeth pulled to clear up the halitosis. You come up with this idea because it's consistent with what you want in life (superior hygiene), and because you are sensitive enough to hear in her suggestions an underlying problem for which you could find a solution.

Listen to people's proposed solutions, but pay most attention to their underlying needs. Then develop the quantum-leap answer to their prayers.

Understand that in your personal life you need to function on two levels:

- First, you need to be sure you have what it takes to fill a genuine need, one you can feel good about filling. This is market awareness.

- Second, you need to convince others to use you to fill their need instead of going elsewhere. This is self-marketing.

You have to provide people with a reason to "buy." This takes guts, persistence, and pizzazz. Selling is tough. But the easier you make it for people to satisfy their needs through you, and the more content you make them feel about the process, the better off you'll both be. When you truly help someone, both of you are materially enhanced.

~~~

TUNING IN TO OTHERS

Successful businesses are sensitive to their customers' needs. Tuning in to cues in your own life as well as those around you produces greater success in your personal life as well.

Sensitivity includes awareness of your own needs and desires, your feelings toward others, your emotional involvement with certain kinds of people, and your attitudes about the overall subject matter. Sensitivity also includes your ability to detect the needs and desires of others and to understand their feelings and emotions. Finally, it means an ability to demonstrate an understanding of what's being said by taking decisive action in your mutual best interests.

Sensitivity requires good listening skills. Use your antennae to "feel" what's behind an issue. Be ready to develop a product or service that is altogether unique in its ability to satisfy an emerging need, one which people are just starting to articulate. As individuals, this means we listen for the dissatisfactions that underlie people's complaints. We continuously experiment with things we can do to ease others' frustrations. We try to remove not only the nagging complaint, but also the subconscious issue underlying it. This means we don't patch up a fight with expensive flowers if our spouse's tension is caused by money worries.

Be sensitive to both the current environment and the future one. Customers know the small improvements they'd like to see, for now. They are unable as a rule, however, to help with new product definitions. That's great for your business today but totally ignores the issue of survival. And it's an issue for which every business and every person is ultimately responsible. Granted, one piece of you must keep up with the demands of today. Keep those current customers happy and satisfied. But it's not enough to keep today's customers happy. How many once-happy customers can you find today for buggy whips? And no matter how ecstatic their customers were, the people who sold whale oil were destined to be put out of business by the kerosene crowd.

Ray Kroc, of McDonald's fame, originally made his living by selling the Multimixer, a device used after World War II to make milkshakes. The McDonald brothers of San Bernardino had eight of Ray Kroc's machines whirling. That was extraordinary. But Ray didn't focus on short-term success; instead, he looked at *why* the McDonald brothers were doing so well. It wasn't because of the Multimixers; it was because the McDonalds were providing a service—fast food—for which there was a growing need. Ray's realization jolted him into a new level of success. He not only listened carefully to what his customers said and didn't say about today's business, but he also sensitized himself to both the current and future business environment. And you should tune in too.

Your environment may give you clues of bad things to come; better to know now than later. Listen carefully to the competition as well. In fact, don't do anything without understanding the customer, the environment, and the competition, as they are evolving. Figure out where they are all headed. That's where you've got to make your play. If it will take you three years to perfect and market your new gizmo, you'd better figure out where all three legs of the stool will be then (customer, environment, and competition). It's like the old football example: the quarterback lets go of the ball so that it will be where the receiver is supposed to be three or four seconds later. Your new creation has to be "on target" for the market that will exist by the time you can deliver your product. In your personal life, this means you probably won't accept a job that requires extensive travel over the next five years if you plan on starting a family next year. Or you won't begin a two-year savings plan for a larger house, when your kids will all be leaving home in another three years. Be sensitive not only to today's needs but also to the ones that lie ahead.

Benefits are those wonderful advantages that accrue to those who "buy" what you have to offer. For firms and for folks, the idea is to find something that will really make a difference to the people who count on you. The difference will draw you closer and provide bona fide satisfaction. It makes them feel good and contributes markedly to their success—and yours.

Be sensitive to your own nature as well. Know what benefits you can deliver.

⧢

SERVING OTHERS

Successful businesses succeed by serving the public. For people too, the payoffs in life are realized by serving others.

This is a foreign concept to some people: Improving our competencies for people who need them makes us more valuable to ourselves as well. All the internal monkeyshines in the world don't solve other people's problems. Corporations and people tend to lose sight of that. We don't exist to make our accountants rich, to build the most impressive corporate office, or to produce thick binders of policies and procedures. By the same token, our personal relationships do not exist for our selfish benefit. Instead, each corporation and individual exists to improve the world in some way—and by so doing, certain mutual benefits will accrue.

The needs you serve cannot be those of your own internal environment. Ultimately, a selfish attitude like this is nonproductive; it will benefit neither you nor the world around you. Instead, you need to focus outside your own concerns. It's easy to fool yourself. As you seek your purpose in life, be careful and honest about your motivation.

A lot of firms talk about being marketing-oriented but end up marketing-*department*-oriented. This is a common, self-serving mistake. In this unfortunate situation, some guru of the "marketing disciplines" pontificates a program he'd like to see his company create for the marketplace.

> SERVICE IS NOT JUST A NOUN, IT'S A VERB. IT'S NOT JUST A JOB, IT'S A CALLING. IT'S NOT JUST A WAY OF DOING BUSINESS, IT'S A PHILOSOPHY OF LIFE.
>
> —DON WARD

Companies that permit such puffery deserve the consequences. In the personal arena, this error is equivalent to thinking that you're generous because you give away free advice to people who don't care what you think.

Companies realize their only hope for survival is to determine what role they want to play in providing a solution to someone else's predicament; they develop that into something tangible and focus on doing at least that one thing very well. And it should be the same with individuals. Everyone has a role as a giver. Service to others builds your net worth—in your own eyes as well as the world's—just as surely as self-centeredness leads to emotional poverty. Figure out how to devote yourself to something that has both meaning and potential for you and yet benefits some larger purpose. When you devote yourself to such service, you will generate long-term payoffs.

Match your skills and goals to someone else's problem. Material rewards will accrue to you—and as you focus on the outside world's need, you will get your internal act together as well. And that feels wonderful.

Imagine you'll wake up tomorrow morning free to choose exactly how you will commit your energies for the rest of your life. Make a list of what you would do. When you're done, ask yourself how many of those purposes you are fully serving today. Consider your actions in light of the key points in chapter three:

- *What needs are you meeting in the world around you with your actions?*
- *Do your actions reinforce a specific service you have to offer to a specific "market" in your life?*
- *Are these actions a response to the actual needs of the people in your life—or are you expecting people to change to suit your needs?*
- *Will these actions be in your best interests? Do you have the resources that will allow you to carry out your intention?*
- *Do these actions initiate interpersonal transactions that will benefit your life?*
- *Does your motivation for these actions spring from your sensitivity to both your internal and external worlds?*
- *What useful purpose will these actions serve? What payoffs do you foresee as a result?*

Four

You can do better— as long as you know what you'd better do

Plan the strategies that will yield payoffs;
find the right road before you set out on the journey.

Some people think they can wander aimlessly, figuring things out as they go along. That's a quick ticket to mediocrity or even disaster. Planning is vital because life is a sea of choices. If we let random currents tug us this way and that, we'll wind up far away from where we want to go.

Be ready for opportunity—but the way you make yourself ready is by choosing a fundamental set of values to guide and sustain you. Use this life philosophy to choose wise actions, especially when the inevitable happens and you find yourself in a situation you never expected. Remember your values. They will take care of your dreams.

Build a rational bridge between your current reality and the life of which you dream. Try to look at the big picture, and don't let your ego or preconceived notions get in the way. Pass up short-term gratification if doing so gets you closer to your goal; wherever you're headed, try not to fly by the seat of your pants. Time spent on planning will pay off gloriously. Choose a path toward success in every role you play. Focus on the future by employing the good business practices that follow.

⤳

HAVING A LIFE PLAN

Successful businesses recognize opportunities by anticipating and planning. You, too, should have a life plan to recognize opportunities and stay focused.

The future can be scary. We're going to have to spend the rest of our lives learning to get comfortable with whatever comes next. How can we know exactly what that will be? We can't. But your next encounter with the awkward unknown is more likely to be successful if you know beforehand what it is that you want and have some idea of how to go about getting it.

Planning is vital. Without it, we tend to leap into action, to do the first thing that occurs to us. Without a plan, we're relegated to the confusion of reacting to other people's demands and priorities. If, however, we free ourselves up to plan for our future, we free ourselves from the bonds of today's reality. Planning gives us a mission, and we carry that commitment with us into every situation and encounter.

The best organizations in the world know they can't possibly predict every circumstance that will come along and preordain the correct response. But they try, and their effort prepares them for a variety of situations. Planning provides businesses with a "vision" against which to test opportunities. If an idea, project, proposal, or deal fits in with that vision, BINGO! If not, they don't waste another minute on it. Planning is no more and no less than a series of priorities and decisions agreed upon in advance.

When you reach a fork in the road, your "plan" keeps you focused on the way you have already decided to turn. Without a plan, both companies and people drift. They have nothing to guide their search for improvement, and they wind up involved with a lot of unproductive or even counterproductive activities. Their time is squandered dealing with today's problems instead of tomorrow's opportunities. Without a plan, without knowing what we're supposed to be doing, every idea, every problem, worry, or opportunity looks the same. We wind up focusing on nothing and constantly switching to whatever is hot today.

Unfortunately, people and companies have a tendency to deal with planning only if nothing really important or really threatening is going on. When things get rough or when a really big fish is on the hook, they suddenly decide they have no time for planning. They drop the discipline and switch back to the seat-of-the-pants approach. That's misguided. A period of crisis is exactly the time to force yourself into more processed thinking. You may be so overwhelmed by a crisis that you feel you don't have time to stop and make a plan, but that's exactly the moment when your judgment is impaired and most of your life experience isn't relevant.

When you are faced with new problems, beware: your "gut feeling" may be out of its league! Your past experience is a poor judge of what to do because the novelty of the situation demands decisions that aren't part of your life history. Because of this human tendency to switch back to seat-of-the-pants mode during a crisis, a lot of poor decisions get made under the false banner of planning. Don't kid yourself like this. Don't pretend you're tackling the tough issues when you're really just darting around willy-nilly. Such foolery will eventually erode your belief in yourself and any process that might help you along. Planning doesn't consume time; it frees up your time. It helps you know what to pass up. And passing up most things is a necessity before you can *do* anything.

The only way for us to end up with something "right" is to plan for it. A lot of bad things can occur with no encouragement whatsoever. The entire history of corporate enterprise bears out that truth, in spades.

Everything about the nature of people and events conspires to drive things toward chaos. Our job is to mold solutions from the confusion. To do so, structure and discipline are required. Whether you're building an atomic submarine, introducing the new Liquid Tide, or putting up your Christmas tree, your results will be more significant, more easily achieved, and more rewarding when you plan for them rather than just leaving it up to fate.

Companies plan in order to gauge what they will be and act like in three, five, or ten years.

> "MOST OF MY IDEAS BELONGED TO OTHER PEOPLE WHO DIDN'T BOTHER TO DEVELOP THEM."
> —THOMAS EDISON

This helps them know how to behave and think today. Their actions now can flow into their intended actions in the future. By glimpsing what they hope to become, they develop a concept of themselves today that is very different from the one they would have otherwise. Without the knowledge of who they are becoming, it's tough for them to know who they are, and therefore how they should act, today. Businesses that plan poorly are always the ones that have trouble deciding priorities, ranking investment opportunities, and focusing their people to work in coordination with one another.

⧢

DREAMING BIG

Successful businesses have dreams and are invigorated when they take steps to realize their dreams. Our best work as well is the work that is inspired by our dreams.

One nice thing about planning is that it affords us the chance to imagine what things will be like if we take steps 1, 2, or 3. It's a powerful concept called visualization. Companies do it all the time. And it works on the personal level as well. For instance, we're told that if you want to lose weight, a first step might be to simply close your eyes and envision yourself thin! As we begin to know what the target looks like, it's easier to tell which actions are consistent with our vision or contrary to attaining it.

To do this, share your ruminations with other people. Daydream, for example, about how good you'll look and feel when you're thinner. Realize the only way you'll ever be satisfied is to reconcile your realities and your fantasies.

Dr. Martin Luther King had a dream. And as he shared his vision with other people, it started to

OUR WILLINGNESS TO CREATE A NEW DREAM OR VISION FOR OURSELVES IS A STATEMENT OF OUR BELIEF IN OUR OWN POTENTIAL.

—DAVID MCNALLY

unfold. Relish your own dreams. Fantasize about what you want. Brainstorm the possibilities. Create scenarios of achievement. Visualize how you will act in order to drive these dreams home. Figure out what actions will and won't work to make your life consistent with achieving your goals. Define yourself as being in the process of making those dreams come true.

Having a dream for your life is the highest form of planning. Your effectiveness will be enhanced because your activities, decisions, and trade-offs will be made in alignment with that dream's guiding principles. Like a compass, your vision for life will keep you pointed in the right direction.

BEING INVOLVED

Successful businesses pay attention to their environment. Likewise, you should be part of the world you inhabit so you are aware of what's happening around you.

This message dates back to the beginnings of Christianity. St. Paul, hardly a wallflower, extolled us to be "in the world." In order to best communicate his message to the early churches of Colossians or Thessalonians, he knew he had to learn enough about those groups to put the message in terms that would resonate with them. Paul knew that to formulate plans we must be part of what's happening in the world in order to connect.

A modern-day example of being "in this world, but not of it" is the Reverend Father Theodore Hesburgh. Although he lived his life contrary to the morals *of* the world, he was still active *in* the world. For thirty-five years, he led the University of Notre Dame from a second-rung academic program to its current preeminence. President Johnson appointed Father Hesburgh to the U.S. Civil Rights Commission, and among the many honors Hesburgh received is the Freedom Medal, the highest citation America can bestow upon a civilian. He has received more honorary doctorate degrees than anyone else in human history.

He's also my personal hero—and a very nice guy! I cherish the photo a friend snapped of Father Hesburgh and me in 1972. His helicopter landed near where we were throwing a Frisbee on the Notre Dame campus and Father Ted jumped out to talk with us. That's not entirely surprising, but the kicker was that the helicopter was delivering Ted Hesburgh back to campus from a board meeting of the Chase Manhattan Bank. Yes, a worldly priest. Not of this world but in it.

In the fiscal year 2000, Notre Dame had the best return on its endowment of any school in the world—almost 60 percent. It's a sizable endowment and beautifully managed; with it a lot of good works can proceed. But strong underpinnings of worldliness were required to transform that sleepy little school in the South Bend snows from a small parochial province of priests to a world-class institution.

Father Hesburgh led the effort to make Notre Dame part of the world—including the 1969 decision to play in bowl games—and the school and the world will never be the same. It remained essentially Catholic, but he turned the school over to a lay board of trustees. The mission remained priestly, but he made sure to bring in the keenest scholars from all over the world.

You'll find that Father Hesburgh's approach will work in your own life as well. Being aware of the world around you opens your mind to brilliant ways to achieve your goals while remaining deeply rooted in your own values. It's a way to take advantage of everything that life offers you, not just the things you happen to bump into.

~

ENLARGING YOUR PERSPECTIVE

Successful businesses see the "big picture." As an individual, let go of any mental framework that distorts or blocks your perspective.

If you can't see the big picture, that doesn't mean it isn't visible. There might be some mindset or filter that clouds your sight. You might be a bit myopic, seeing only the tree, not the forest. Work to improve your vision. Take off the blinders or the shades. See what's really out there. Do whatever it takes to get a better perspective. If necessary, seek a new paradigm; find a fresh way to approach the view.

The three men in the list below all grasped the big picture. Pretend you're in third grade; get out a pencil and draw a line from the name in the first column to the creation in the second column for which they are famous.

Henry Ford	the electric light
Thomas Edison	the steamboat
Robert Fulton	the automobile

Okay, I assume you each got 100 percent on the test, and you are ready for what comes next.

You're right, Henry Ford is famous for his automobile, but he is far more famous because of his automobile company! Henry was not even one of the first people in the world to invent a car. Yes, he was inventive. He made his first gasoline engine in 1893 and his first vehicle in 1896. But Gottlieb Daimler and Karl Benz had each developed engines of the type used today years before, in 1885. The Duryea brothers had perfected a gasoline-powered automobile in 1893. In 1896, when Ford introduced his car, three others had models to show as well: Alexander Winton, Ransom Eli Olds, and Charles Brady King. What made Henry famous was the way in which he manufactured and sold his cars.

Henry was quick to figure out that if he wanted a leg up on his competitors, he couldn't focus on the expensive autos that were the rage at the time. Instead, he developed a system of mass-producing cars that allowed him to cut his costs and produce a reliable and sturdy vehicle that middle-class Americans could afford. The savings enjoyed as the result of Henry's assembly line system allowed him to drop his price to his customers and made his company the leading automobile producer of the first half of the twentieth century. Henry created a profit-sharing plan for his employees, cut the length of the workday, and paid workers at the Ford Motor Company more than double what they could earn in similar Detroit jobs. He got the pick of the best applicants, and together the people of the Ford Motor Company made Henry famous for the automobile.

How about Edison? It's almost the same story. He is famous for the light bulb, but he was not the first to invent it. Edison was nonetheless brilliant and remains the most prolific inventor in American history. But the fact is that when he completed the work on his incandescent prototype in 1879, a Russian engineer named

Paul Jablochkov had already lit up a Paris street with arc lights two years earlier. One competitor, Joseph Swann, developed another very successful prototype.

Edison's response was to buy up the patents and incorporate Swann's ideas into his own factories. That's right, factories. While many other brilliant people were working to make a single prototype that would work, Edison was figuring out how to manufacture bulbs at a profit. And Edison went on. Not only did he figure out how to efficiently manufacture the lights, he designed a whole system through which electricity could be routed safely to homes and other businesses. Always the inventor, Edison did not stop (or even start) with the light bulb. He created a delivery system for all things electrical and had financing lined up so he could roll out his lines quickly and beat his competitors. Edison wasn't a schoolboy with a bright idea, taking his odd brainstorms from investor to investor to see if anyone would buy them. He created what would become the General Electric Company! Edison realized that without a stream of electricity, bulbs were of no value. Thomas Edison had the big picture.

You see the pattern? Robert Fulton's 1807 creation, the *Clermont*, was not the first steamship. That distinction was won by John Finch in 1787. But Fulton's was the first commercial success, running 150 miles up the Hudson from New York to Albany in 30 hours. Finch built a brilliant curiosity; Fulton created a steamship company that allowed the concept to spread, building his reputation and writing the history you learned in third grade.

The winners, they say, write history. I'm sure that Messrs. Jablochkov, Finch, et al. were every bit as bright and industrious as Ford, Edison, and Fulton. But the latter three all created systems of production and delivery. They spent as much time on the commercial application of their idea as on the invention itself. They understood that it made no difference if they had an automobile, light bulb, or steamship if there were no factories, power lines, or passengers. They backed away from their favorite project long enough to see how it fit in the whole mosaic. They saw the big picture. History has made up the rest.

Those who command the big picture must train themselves to see how unfolding events can fit together later. They use friends, competitors, customers, and media to see which way things are going—and then they create ways to intersect happily with the events just beginning to transpire. The big picture isn't having the best idea, the best implementation, or the best of anything. It is seeing how things fit together now, and imagining how things will fit together in the future.

People who see the big picture look at the mosaic, not at the little ceramic squares. If by a twist of fate, they find themselves to be makers of little squares, they paint verbal pictures about all the magical things that can come from the creative use of those squares. They see what is possible and help their customers see it, too. They make it easy to order, ship, and use the squares, and even develop tools, templates, and tutorials to help the users of the little squares get started. They inspire would-be mosaic makers to greatness.

And so it is in your life. Your creations may be brilliant. You may be brilliant, but the intended users may not be. That user sometimes may be your boss. Bosses have other things to do than figure out how to make you a hero through the implementation of your fabulous idea. If no one is moved by your ideas or creations, it may be that you haven't helped people to adopt or implement your concept. Having the big picture requires you not just to be bright and creative; it also asks that you make it easy for others in your life to say "yes" to your ideas.

Seeing the big picture is seldom easy and not always necessary. For the most part we view life through a framework that filters information, helping us focus on the details—the ceramic tiles—that make the big picture possible. The fact is, we need the big picture only once in awhile. We don't need it every second. We don't even need it every day. In fact, if we spent our lifetimes cogitating on large, broad thoughts, we wouldn't be even remotely successful.

Think of your need for perspective in terms of the American bald eagle. What a beautiful creature, and what a successful creature. The eagle is an exceptionally good hunter, highly skilled, quick, and gracefully powerful. It doesn't succeed by sitting on its nest. It takes to the sky to survey the situation, and having reached its zenith in the heavens, it spends time "checking out" the lay of the land. Only when it spots an opportunity does it swoop down on its prey. In those moments, it is riveted, fiercely focused, even single-minded. Occasionally, though, it must back away from the matters close at hand to get the perspective needed to sight its aim and hone its skills. The big picture isn't necessary every moment, but when it is, *it is*.

We, like the eagle, must find a way to gain perspective away from the day-to-day hubbub, without filters and frameworks. We have to look around until we really see what is going on . . . and then we can swoop in for the kill. We can then focus intensely on the work we need to get done.

The greatest obstacle to seeing the big picture is egocentricity. Our worldview causes us to filter and block so much that we miss seeing the actual world. Our set of beliefs determines in advance how we will see things. We pigeonhole others, classifying them religiously, politically, and socially, and we fail to see them as they really are.

This is why it's easy to tell where any map of the world was printed. The ones in every U.S. classroom I've ever seen have North America in the middle. All the other countries are shown sprawled out to the east, west, north, and south of us. Although the children are learning where other countries are in relation to their own, it's easy to think as though our nation were at the center of the universe. We tend to think everything revolves around us, which isn't accurate. It's abject egocentrism, and it's the dominant element of what keeps us from seeing the big picture. We belong not only to a single country but an entire planet. We can no longer pretend that events on the other side of that planet have no influence on our daily lives.

Pope Urban II was guilty of this in a horrible way. During the age of the Crusades he sent thousands of European men and boys to their deaths because he failed to see the big picture. The Crusades were based on the faulty assumption that the Muslims were ignorant and savage pagans who would fall easily. This view saw *us* as right, therefore powerful, and *them* as evil weaklings who would be quickly defeated. Egocentricity blinded the medieval church and the foolish kings who fell in with the church's assumptions. The ripple effect of their actions is still being felt in our world today.

Egocentric thinking continues to distort the worldview of many of us, including business leaders. We expect some magic will occur to ensure prosperity, protect us from tumult, or deliver our pathetic competitors mercilessly to our feet. But we cannot make wise plans if we fail to see the entire picture.

BEING CONSISTENT WITH TOMMORROW'S GOALS

Successful businesses consistently reinvest short-term profits to reap the maximum long-term rewards. You, too, should think, dream, and act today consistently with what you want for tomorrow.

No sane executive would tell you to go just for the short-term gains. There are plenty of opportunities to grab the quick fix, the short-term gain, the immediate gratification. The best companies resist these temptations with as much vigor and commitment as they can muster. It takes discipline.

But good companies know the inclination to book short-term profits would, if continued, preclude their ability to invest in new business opportunities. It's like the shortsighted farmer who eats the seed corn. What will he do next year? When in doubt, do what will be good for your future. Live intensely and alertly in today. Keep your seed corn well protected.

> THE FUTURE CANNOT BE PREDICTED, BUT FUTURES CAN BE INVENTED. IT IS OUR ABILITY TO INVENT THE FUTURE THAT GIVES US HOPE AND MAKES US WHAT WE ARE.
> —DENNIS GABOR

Do what you do for the long-term payoff. That includes, by the way, staying healthy and profitable today. A dejected workaholic who reaps none of the benefits of her work today isn't likely to enjoy them later, either. Ask yourself the long-term effects of today's alternatives.

For instance, ten years from now your life probably won't be much different if you choose tonight to clear your desk before you quit for the day. But if you opt instead to go home and spend some time with your spouse or carry through on an exercise program or pursue a new talent, these decisions may well have a significant impact on your quality of life ten years in the future.

Once you've decided what you want, then you must decide what you will have to give up in order to get what you want. You must use that information to make strategic sacrifices, but with an eye toward the big payoff down the road. Your sacrifices should always be in service of achieving something bigger or deeper later. Companies eke out enough pleasure to get them through the day all the while supporting their long-term goals. You, personally, should allow yourself enough pleasure to keep you motivated, while simultaneously sacrificing for your long-term goals.

Your decisions about when to take your payoffs are often just a matter of style or preference. Sometimes, though, the immediate payoff is deleterious. We all know not to eat and drink too much or overindulge in other ways. The short-term payoffs of such behaviors are counterproductive to our long-term well-being.

It's hard sometimes for even the most seasoned CEO to pass up short-term profits in favor of the long-term gain. The stockholders, the employees, the banks, and just about every other constituency associated with the firm want it to be at its most profitable *today*. You, too, will experience this problem. In virtually every role you fill, you'll encounter people who want you to consume and spend the relationship instead of saving and investing in it. Find ways to creatively resist. You may even have to look bad for a while in the eyes of your significant others. So, look bad. Your long-term success will eventually vindicate you. The oft-spotted bumper sticker on the old VW beetle tells it well: "It ain't much, but it's paid for." Don't let the crowd get you down. They may not be around later if you need help. Do what's right for the future, even if it means looking bad today.

Think long term—and live the short term consistent with that vision. Use broad brushstrokes to color your future—but don't paint yourself into a corner by ignoring what's around you now. Live out the details of your life today in ways that support your dream for tomorrow.

⤬

DEFINING YOUR SUCCESS

Wise executives define a company's concept of success. You, too, should define success, so you'll know what it looks like.

How we play the game depends on how we define success. What does it mean to succeed? Who are we and what will we do? How will we know when we have been successful? Will hitting our goals by thirty-five be terrific? If it takes us until we're fifty, will we be failures?

We become what we dream of being not through some enormous and dramatic one-time effort but because of hundreds of small everyday decisions that support our goals. If we can't realistically define ourselves as Olympic gold medalists, we can still be the best in our age group, the best in our class, the best we are within striking distance of being. We all want to strive, to grow, and to succeed. But if we define ourselves as having to beat Michael Jordan at rebounds, we're just setting ourselves up for failure. We need to strive simply to be the best we can be. That starts out by understanding ourselves and what we want and working from there.

Success is relative. For a company, the ultimate success is to be generating the highest return on invested capital. For us as individuals, it's achieving our highest potential using the talents and gifts we have been given. But be careful. Both businesses and people can fall into perilous traps while defining success.

In the first trap, we may measure our performance against last year's or against how we did last time we were up at bat. Be careful. Just because you're beating yourself doesn't mean you're doing well. If you were a bad poet last year, are you more successful because your recent poetry is only half as bad?

In the second snare, businesses and people routinely compare themselves only against the competition. Here again, just because you're beating someone else today doesn't mean you are in fact performing anywhere near your potential.

So what is the answer? Half the self-help advisers agree with President Eisenhower, an avid golfer, who said you should "shoot against your own par." The other half agree with legendary football coach Vince Lombardi, who said "winning isn't everything; it is the *only* thing." I agree with both of these statements and neither of them. The key to defining success for yourself is to use timeless values and principles that apply for a particular period of time for a specific opportunity.

You don't have to be perfect; you just have to be better than the rest. Perfection has too high a cost. It is important to know when something is good enough. To use the school example once again, the winner of the third-grade spelling bee wasn't really all that great a whiz—she was just better than the other third-graders. In order to be a perfect speller she would have had to sacrifice other schoolwork. The cost of being perfect wouldn't be worth it since being better than the others was all she needed to win the bee. Strengths are relative, and if you are better than, that's enough. However, avoid the trap mentioned in the last chapter and don't sacrifice maximizing your potential at the altar of lousy competition.

Lever Brothers and Colgate can and do make a world of claims and counterclaims about their competitive brands in the marketplace. Neither firm, however, can afford to supply the "perfect" product. Both firms know how to make their products technically superior in one area or another, but they also know nobody is willing to pay for perfection. Life is a series of tradeoffs. The company that makes the sale is the one who is better than the rest. It will never be perfect.

If you position your strengths to convince people that you are the solution to their problems, then you want to be seen as someone who stacks up favorably to the others in your area of expertise. Your ability to do the next job gets compared to that of the others in the heap. You don't have to be the best in the world; you only need to be better than the others in the rat race you are trying to win. That will be hard enough.

Eisenhower was right: a business should push itself to do better today than it did yesterday and avoid focusing too much on what other businesses—or people—are doing. Why? For one thing, you cannot control what your competitors do or do not do. You cannot control what opportunities will fall in their laps or what devastation might strike them. You cannot control their time frames or time pressures, and you certainly cannot control their values or principles.

You can't conclude that Eisenhower didn't consider winning important. I'm sure he didn't feel that way on D-Day, 1944, when he led the Normandy invasion. The whole world was counting on us to win Europe back from the Nazis. Eisenhower's advice is simply that we need to focus every day on doing better than we ever have before. On D-Day, we definitely did so. Eisenhower was stressing that we should all commit to a life of constant improvement. This ageless value drives particular actions appropriate to win the moment and do better than we did yesterday.

Now let's look again at Lombardi's quote about winning being everything. During his nine years as head coach and general manager of the Green Bay Packers, he won an amazing five NFL titles. But that also means he failed to win four. Do you think he just slithered away in shame after these losses? No. He used his mistakes to figure out how to win next time. Losing doesn't make you a loser. It may be the first step toward winning in the future.

All our definitions of success must take these conclusions into account:

1. Any success is situational.

2. Any success is relative.

3. Any success is temporary.

Because success is situational, we know that our finest accomplishment in one of our roles may not make the slightest difference in our other roles. Just because we have an Oscar doesn't mean we can speed on the freeway and not get stopped by a state trooper. If we stand out as an actor, we need to save it for the screen; the policeman may not be impressed with our theatrics.

Because success is relative, we know that being the best of the worst may not win any big awards, but it may be all we need. The fastest swimmer in the pool at the time wins the meet. If everyone is having a bad day, one swimmer still gets the blue ribbon. But other competitors are swimming in other pools right this minute, so we need to define our success not from without but from within. We must do our best with what we have been given and push ourselves every day to train and improve. We must also learn to define our success in terms of what we have done with what we were given. There will always be someone bigger, stronger, faster, richer or better looking. That needn't discourage us if we define our success in such a way that we can stretch ourselves, improve ourselves, and keep growing, while accepting the unbelievably talented and gifted people who share this planet with us. We can't beat ourselves up for losing to Mark Spitz.

Because success is temporary, we need to do all we can to identify new ways to continue a run of successes. This is something winning companies do brilliantly. A good corporation continues its existence long after any single product or business rises or falls. The corporation's life ends only if it fails to renew itself by serving new and emerging needs. For example, IBM did not start as a computer company; it had a slew of product innovations before it had anything that could be considered a "computer," and it has introduced many generations of products since then. This company could have died nine deaths already. It hasn't because it has found vibrant new ways to extend its life cycle. People need to do that as well. Sometimes our roles fade. Sometimes our ideas die. Sometimes what we do is no longer of value to people. Sometimes we have to figure out a new way to relate to the world or we will just shrivel up and go away. Because success is a fleeting thing, we have to recognize that today's success will not sustain us forever. We must strive to find ways to extend the satisfaction we derive from our recent successes by seeking new places where we can shine.

Back in 1964, the wealthiest man in the history of the state of Tennessee (though he wasn't that yet) bought a sagging little schoolbook company. Bronson Ingram got a pretty good deal, but it still turned out to be a rather drab little business. Most of the sales came during a small window in the late summer, and the customers were the staid members of state and county textbook adoption committees. Not exactly the kind of rip-roarin' business Bronson dreamed of owning. But, as modest as he always was, that man was a genius. (I know because I had the good fortune to work with him for many years.) Bronson Ingram took that boring little outfit and built it into one of the largest privately held companies in the world. He did it by formulating a new definition for bookselling success.

First, he looked for ways to spread the sales of the product beyond the seasonal corner of summer. He brought in some bestsellers and classic trade books and began to stock titles from various publishers. Back in those days, arranging to have a book shipped from a publisher to your little bookstore was like ordering a piece of custom furniture from a North Carolina factory. It could take forever. Bronson had the idea of gathering up books from different publishers in one warehouse and offering them year-round to retailers. That was a hugely different definition of the business from what was served up to him when he bought the Tennessee schoolbook depository. His ingenuity gave birth to the Ingram Book Company.

Bronson understood that the bookstores needed to find out what books were available or he wouldn't be able to help them. So he hired a young marketing man from Bell & Howell who seemed to have the kind of customer orientation needed to make the business a success. Harry Hoffman was everything Ingram wanted, but in a stroke of serendipity, he had another unusual skill: Harry knew the ins and outs of microfiche technology. Through microfiche, libraries and research institutes were able to keep ponderous amounts of data on very small plastic plates. Hoffman immediately saw that Ingram could put its inventory onto fiche, and then sell a retailer a microfiche reader and a subscription to the fiche, including the regular updates of inventory available.

This innovation turned the book business on its ear in the early 1970s. Now the distributor was packaging information along with the product, charging for it, and making a bundle! And it was all due to the happy fact that Bronson did not define his success in a traditional way.

Bronson passed away in 1995, and I still miss him. However, his commitment to continuous and relevant redefinition continues to influence the companies that bear his name. From the rib of Ingram Book Company two industry titans have sprung, also born of redefining moments: Ingram Entertainment (which I named, and then ran for several years as Chief Operating Officer), the world's largest distributor of prerecorded videocassettes; and Ingram Micro, which serves the same purpose in the field of computer software and peripherals. The total market value of the Ingram companies exceeded $4 billion by the late 1990s.

Bronson knew how to define success. He didn't allow himself to be restricted by traditional definitions for his industry. When you define what you mean by success, it can be the most productive thing you ever do. How we define success defines how we progress!

Businesses don't achieve their definition of success by accident, and they don't just sit back and wait for success to happen. Instead, the strategies they choose help them take advantage of the opportunities that come along. Their dreams for the future are firmly based on the real world's long-term big picture.

You, too, can choose a path to success. So do it.

Now!

Think about the moments in your life—we have all had these moments—when you were "brilliant" but not successful. Where in the planning and execution processes did you "miss it?" Evaluate your actions in light of the key points in chapter four:

- *Did you have a life plan in place?*
- *Were you inspired by a dream or vision for the future?*
- *Were you paying attention to cues from the world around you?*
- *Did you grasp the big picture?*
- *Were you looking at short-term effects and missing the long-term perspective?*
- *How had you defined success?*

How will you adjust your strategies next time?

Five

THE CLUB YOU NEED IS
ALREADY IN YOUR BAG

Deploy assets for maximum advantage;
make the most of the blessings you enjoy in each role.

The club you need, along the back nine of everyday life, could be a sand wedge, a driver, or a putter. Life drops us into the rough sometimes—and into the occasional trap as well. Sometimes we're swinging away with all our might, rolling down the fairway. Other times we need to use careful calculation and a soft touch to move straight and true toward the cup.

Know yourself and your skills, and don't be afraid to get help from people who have played the course before. Pick the right club, and hit that shot with the talent and finesse you know you possess. Your success is already in the bag.

✍

COUNTING YOUR ASSETS

Successful businesses know their resources. You, too, should count your blessings and know how to use them.

Businesses count their inventories. People, instead, tend to count all the things they *don't* have, but again, business has this one right. You will do better if you recognize and use all the things you have going for yourself. Quietly appreciate yourself and focus your strengths into a useful force that will produce dramatic results.

Even with the best of luck, skill, and gusto, it's crazy to proceed without the command of all of the tools available to you. If you're healthy, if you have people who love you, if you have self-respect plus the respect of other people, or if you have ideas, skills, talents, and energy, you have some very important assets. Control your resources to create opportunities through which you can shine.

If you're going into the job market, for example, you need to use the inventory process. Think about the things you do well and where those skills would fit. Create a document, with one page listing your strengths and another listing your weaknesses. The first page can help you write your résumé, leveraging your strengths to build your case for being hired. Keep the second page in your back pocket; you should be able to demonstrate how and why these weaknesses are non-issues.

Whether you're looking for a new job or not, you need a constant inventory of where your strengths lie. You need to maximize those strengths in each of your roles. What's more, today's assets will become your future. So, take the time to write them down. You need to understand what you clearly command in the form of resources and assets. These could fill pages. Once you have your inventory complete, you can figure out what you can borrow from other people.

This borrowing takes two forms. One is approaching other people to barter and trade some of what you have for some of what you need. Your relationships with others allow you to match up with other people's assets. That lets you get the job done. Share generously, borrow liberally, trade creatively, and barter indefatigably. Get in touch with what you really know about people and what they want.

The second is going back and getting in touch with what other people have already learned. Read the biographies of famous and successful people. See what helped them get over the real-life situations that are bothering you now. Determine what they did to act on their ideas. Make use of those ideas yourself.

Almost every business school trains its students to use the "case method." That is, students learn lessons from businesses that have already dealt with a particular situation, good or bad. After all, millions and millions of folks have gone before us. They have uncovered a great deal about science, relationships, and themselves, and they have written down wonderful testimonies of their discoveries. Draw liberally from what literature and science texts tell us. Talk with people. Gather ideas. One of the things businesses do well is to tap into trade associations and databases, resources that would be very expensive to develop independently. They share information, and entire industries get bigger, better, and more profitable.

A tenet of new product development is to avoid the "not invented here" trap. It's called NIH thinking. Many people, given a challenge to come up with a new toy car, for example, will spend weeks creating new little rubber tires that they simply could have bought from other companies with inventories of such components. If certain parts of the product aren't unique, it's better to go out and buy these parts, focusing the energy, talent, and resources of the designers on developing what *will* be new and exciting about the toy.

If we can borrow (or buy) what's already available, we can focus our energies on the unique and exciting work we are dedicated to achieving. This kind of thinking also helps us understand that what we can't do well isn't really important. Yes, as I said in the last chapter, we need to understand our weaknesses, but only to the extent that they limit our strengths. It's a total waste of time to worry about your weakness in making little rubber wheels if somebody out there can make wheels for you.

As you inventory your resources to find the ones that will help you reach your goals, you'll also find ones that aren't useful. Unless those resources are important to your future, they are just curiosities; divest them. Free your time and energy for focusing on what really matters to you.

Have you ever worked somewhere and felt you could do more, that your skills weren't being utilized? Your superiors could have done you and themselves a favor if they had sat down with you and discussed the company's mission and how your talents might or might not fit in. Both you and the employer could have focused your energies on steering you to a better job, inside or outside the company, that would use your talents more fully. Failing to use an asset is a sad thing.

Mark Twain said, "The man who does not read good books is at no advantage over the man who can't read them." If you're not using a particular skill or resource you possess, you might as well not have it at all.

⚬

ACCEPTING GOODWILL

In the business world, good customers—goodwill—is the lifeblood of a company. In our personal lives, the goodwill of others is an extremely valuable asset.

A business's group of loyal customers is an asset. It can be measured, assigned a value, and used to borrow cash against. When acquisitions are being made or divestitures contemplated, the customer base and its loyalty is always a deciding factor in the price of the deal.

Several times in my career I have been responsible for integrating large companies into our own after mergers. Although we paid for accounts receivable, inventories, fixed assets, and certain contractual obligations into which we wanted to enter, what really excited us—what we *actually* bought—was a pool of dedicated people who had strong and growing relationships with customers. People and their relationships are what produce value.

Goodwill is an asset you can control in your personal life as well. You can make it bigger by focusing on the importance of relationships, or you can allow it to dwindle through neglect. Relationships not only guide and mold you, but ultimately they define you. Wealth isn't just the dollars you have in the bank; in many cases it's your connections. Your next role, your next idea, your next opportunity will depend on many, many relationships. Don't deny the importance of goodwill, whether it shows up on your balance sheet or not.

Remember *The Godfather*? Don Corleone's career was effective because he went out and did good deeds for people, favors upon which he could later collect. Now I'm not suggesting you call in your favors the way he did or deal with people who disappoint you the way he did. But the basic concept of goodwill is a balancing act. Do a good deed for someone, and that person will usually want to help you in return. That doesn't mean you should look at each of your relationships in a manipulative, self-serving way. But you should be aware of the way things work. If you're fair to others, they'll be more apt to be fair to you. Conversely, if you treat them poorly, that will come back to haunt you.

Relationships are one of your greatest assets, because through them you will understand people and what they want. Knowing what people want and talking with them about it will help you discover what would satisfy their needs. And that's a goldmine. Time and time again in my career, it has been the tip from the field, the phone call from the airport, or the quick hand-jotted note from someone who cared about me or my company that allowed me to seize opportunities that were unfolding.

Businesses know that most customers won't complain about the things you do wrong. So if you do get one complaint, you'd better figure five more are out there, people who don't think it's worth their time to tell you they aren't happy. Their orders will just decline, and they will go away quietly.

It's the same with the people in your personal life. Pay attention to any hints you get that people are unhappy with your behavior. If you want others to be respectful and truthful with you, don't do things that others may find obnoxious, and don't do things that will keep people from telling you the truth. You want people to feel comfortable

> MOST OF US NEVER QUALIFY FOR LIFE'S GRAND AWARDS—NO OSCAR, EMMY, OR NOBEL PRIZE. BUT WE ALL HAVE A SHOT AT ONE WORTHWHILE PURSUIT—THE CHANCE TO DELIVER QUALITY IN ALL THAT WE DO FOR OTHERS.
> —DAN ZADRA

enough to tell you what you could do to improve yourself or to help them improve themselves. This is the way to establish deep and growing relationships.

When it comes to determining assets, I like the expression "getting the most bang for your buck" better than the phrase "the bottom line." I prefer not to talk in terms of the bottom line because it suggests a very short-term orientation. It gives no suggestion of the many relationships that go into defining and executing a business proposition.

Most companies, especially ones that are bottom-line oriented pay lip service to asset utilization, but instead they behave as though profitability and return on sales are the only true measures. This is, of course, hogwash. Goodwill never shows up on a profit-and-loss statement, so bottom-line oriented managers and companies tend to miss it altogether when they evaluate their resources.

The most effective businesspeople I know understand that they have to get the most bang for their bucks, and those are the people who make sure to share information with their trade associations. Those are the people who leverage off good relationships and information, who trade and borrow assets, and generally use what they have to get what they need. They depend on their goodwill as one of their most essential assets.

You, also, should leverage good relationships. If you want to be friends with someone or develop a relationship with someone, work on the goodwill factor. Get to know their interests and play to them. If your son likes rap music and you want to cultivate a relationship there, learn something about the music and culture. Don't buy him a fishing pole for Christmas when he really wants to go to a rap concert. Wear some earplugs and take him to the show. Developing goodwill takes paying attention to the details and will go a long way in your personal relationships.

~

MAXIMIZING YOUR RELATIONSHIPS

Successful businesses maximize their productivity before they seek out new enterprises. You, too, should maximize the relationships you already have before entering new ones.

The way to get the most out of life is to find out what you have today that you can use to get something more. The word to describe this concept is productivity. For businesses, productivity means almost everything. Unfortunately, many companies focus on new ventures to increase profits when there are opportunities in their own backyard to dramatically improve efficiency and productivity. Improving productivity should be management's first goal, before it tries to develop new markets and new products. Since you control all the variables, it's far less risky to work on efficiency than it is to take new money and play it out in the marketplace with a plan that may or may not succeed.

For instance, some companies are obsessed with reducing the payroll. Better companies look at payroll not as an expense but as an investment. Of course, reducing payroll will always be one aspect of management, but I would suggest that going out and making the people you have more productive is far more important than getting rid of some of them.

A business that works to increase the productivity of its people—through improved training, careful communication of the mission, understanding morale, sharing information, and developing a safe and productive work environment—is far more likely to increase profitability than a competitor who either slashes its people or rushes out to grab a new market without having its own internal act together. The disciplined control of resources operates to create opportunity and productivity, and then takes on an entirely new meaning.

Apply these principles to your personal life as well. For instance, if you're not happy with the payoff you're receiving from the relationships in your life, before you run out looking for entirely new friends and lovers, try maximizing the potential of the relationships you already have. Invest your time and energy to determine what the people in your life need. Listen to them and be willing to try new things. If we assume there's probably a better way to do almost everything—because after all, we're not smart enough to have thought of everything—we create an attitude that fosters open-mindedness, growth, and resourcefulness.

This is not only the efficient way to run the operation—or a relationship—that exists today; it's also the way to help finance the dream of tomorrow. It's the bridge between making money and saving money. The efficient use of assets creates the pool of resources that will be used to finance the next opportunity.

Many companies positively reinforce their management for protecting resources. The best ones, however, reinforce their people for identifying the resources they already command and coming up with exciting new uses for them. Productivity increases when employees have a mission, a context, and a direction. It's management's job to provide this for an organization, but it's your job to find it for yourself.

You may have heard the story of the stonecutter and the cathedral builder:

A passerby stopped a man who was chiseling a block of stone and asked what he was doing. The man replied that he was cutting stone. The passerby moved on to a second man chiseling stone. Asked the same question, the second man said he was building a cathedral.

The stonecutter and the cathedral builder may look like they are doing the same job, but I guarantee you they experience their work very differently. If management makes the people on the job feel like cathedral builders, it creates a body of people that want to execute their tasks more efficiently so that the larger work can take place.

Quantum leaps in productivity can be achieved just by thinking about the world differently. You too need to find a mission and a vision that will increase your personal productivity. Even the most menial tasks—like scrubbing a toilet or taking out the family garbage—contribute to an overarching grander goal. Keep your eyes on your ultimate mission. When you do, you can use the resources you have today as efficiently as you can to build your dreams for your future.

⤫

INVESTING YOUR TIME

Successful businesses recognize that time is a resource that must be conserved. Your time is a precious asset as well, and you'd better invest it wisely.

If you don't know what time it is, you don't know whether to bob or weave, run or punt, fish or cut bait. Wise choices are intertwined with exceptional timing. *When* we ask or act can be as critical as *what* we ask or do.

In the depth of our beings ticks a biological clock, which knows that every project and plan has a gestation period that can't be overruled. A certain amount of time is required to go from idea to reality. However, over the length of our lives we can probably accomplish more than we think. Yet in a day we can accomplish less than we want to admit.

> PEOPLE SAY, WHAT IS THE SENSE OF OUR SMALL EFFORTS? THEY CANNOT SEE WE MUST LAY ONE BRICK AT A TIME.
> —DOROTHY DAY

Somehow the immediacy of the present makes us nearsighted. It's that forest-for-the-trees thing again: focusing on today's trees, we miss tomorrow's forest. We have at least one thing right, though: today is the day we have some time to use. And today, we better decide to focus our time on the life we want to have. If we don't invest our time in the things that are important to our lives as a whole, we will not only waste our time, but we will squander our lives!

You see, time is the scarcest resource. With it you can make all the others. Failing to use it wisely keeps you from using any other resource well.

Here's what the great economist Adam Smith said in 1776: "The real price of everything, what everything really costs to the man who wants to acquire it, is the toil and trouble of acquiring it." And "toil and trouble" take time. That's why when a business chooses between two economic options, the corporate chieftains always consider the amount of time that each plan would absorb. Businesses have to ask, "Could this time be better invested in another project that would return a buck more quickly?"

As an individual, the tricky thing about investing your time is that you don't really know how much you have. You can reasonably figure what your net worth might be, and calculate what the value might be in five or thirty-five years. But you have no idea how much time you actually have left. With other resources, you know when you are nearing the bottom of the barrel. Not with time. You can't plan to spend your last two years with your grandchildren in the same way you can plan how to spend your last two dollars.

We must be accountable for how we use our time today. Any given slice of any day needs to reflect our goals in life. Today should be a microcosm of how we'd like our epitaphs to read. If we want to stay healthy, we need to eat wisely and exercise—today. If we want to be developing our minds, we need to read the type of writing that will expand us intellectually—today. If we want to be better spouses, we need to reach out and do something exceptionally generous for our lovers—today.

We can't stockpile our time to spend tomorrow, and we can't afford to go to the grave with good intentions.

It's not a crime to lie in a shaded hammock on a summer afternoon and watch the boats float down the river. Such a thing can replenish and invigorate you. That's good. I'm not saying you

> ARE WE WILLING TO GIVE UP SOME THINGS WE LIKE TO DO, IN ORDER TO MOVE ON TO THOSE THINGS WE MUST DO?
> —SATENIG ST. MARIE

should be an unrelenting automaton who never slows down or takes a rest. A restful day can be happily spent with one's family; rekindling the heart in quiet solitude can be equally rejuvenating. Although at first glance these activities may seem "nonproductive," these are actually wonderful uses of time. They are consistent with life goals and will be smiled upon in old age. On the other hand, sitting in front of the TV all day is a nonproductive waste of time. You know when you have "blown" a day, putting nothing into it and getting nothing out of it.

There are many things you can focus on today that are good and wholesome, consistent with the person you are trying to become. When conflicting goals present themselves, and you can't decide what to do, pick one—the highest one on your hierarchy of roles—and get started with it. Just do the next thing you know you have to do that is good for you and your goals. The vista will clear, you'll stand on higher ground, and what you ought to do next will become more obvious. It may turn out on Monday morning that it wasn't the very best choice, but at least you'll have pointed yourself in the right direction.

General George S. Patton said, "I would rather have a good plan today than a perfect plan two weeks from now." Timing really is everything. Where Mozart put rests in his compositions turns out to be as important as the melody. Where Faulkner puts a semicolon tells us the tempo of the literary page. And where Jay Leno pauses before a punch line may mean the difference between laughs and a bust.

Nicolaus Copernicus, who lived from 1473 to 1543, knew the importance of timing as well. He refused to release the great work of his lifetime until he was quite certain he was dying. In 1543, he published his heliocentric model of the solar system—and then he died. He knew the furor the theory would create. If his ideas had come out while he was alive, he and his family might have suffered. But after his death everyone was curious to hear his theory. The scientific community was eager to see what he had to say. How do you argue with a dead man?

As teenagers, we used to be pretty good at this matter of timing. We knew not to interrupt Dad during the game to ask for the car keys, and we knew the order in which to tell our story when we were half an hour late getting home. We still know these things, but we tend to think that what we want is so important that we can blurt it out at any time and expect an accommodating audience. Forget it. If research on consumer behavior has taught the companies of America anything, it's that when you deliver the message is as important as what you say.

For example, no company that has its act together would announce the release of its new software before it has been thoroughly tested and debugged for shipping. To do so would make the current version obsolete on retail shelves before there's something new to replace it—and that would hand precious retail space to the competition. Yet as individuals, many of us will announce a change prematurely, burning our bridges before we have surveyed the road across the next chasm.

Another thing we can learn from business about timing comes from the world of negotiation. People in corporate offices spend a lot of time talking about when to make a move. For example, a company may go to its landlord two years before the lease expires to talk about an extension, new floor coverings, or better lighting in the parking lots. At this point you still have two years to find another location if the two of you can't come to terms. This gives you greater leverage. If you wait until four months before your lease expires, the landlord knows it would be a miracle for you to find a new location in time, and your power in the negotiation dissipates. Timing is everything. Spend time on your timing.

Businesses also know how hard it is to get a consumer to switch brands, but smart companies know customers are more open to it at certain times. When companies are merging, customer loyalty tends to be at a low ebb. The name of the company often changes. Furthermore, as management tries to make the merged operations uniform, it may make changes that inconvenience the customers. Service levels may be at their worst due to confusion about who is doing what. The big new company that just spent millions to put a deal together has actually become more vulnerable. This isn't the time to push for new customers. Better companies know to hit home the sales message when they are in a less vulnerable position at the same time that customers are less happy with the competitor.

The same applies to you. Present your ideas or your availability for a new job when the decision makers are most dissatisfied with the current state of affairs. You don't have to swim upstream. You are not a salmon. It is perfectly okay to hit the target when it wants to be hit. But it will take timing. For example, if your wife is overwhelmed with a project at work, that is not the time to ask her to have a romantic lunch with you. On the other hand, if she hasn't seen you in a week and a half because of sales meetings, that would be the perfect time to plan a weekend getaway. So strike while the iron is hot and mold a new future. Another example is waiting for the right moment to teach your child something. Sadly, these opportunities often come when the child is hurting. They are quiet. They are experiencing enough pain or disquietude that they are willing to put aside the way they are doing things in order to listen for a short time to an alternative. Timing is everything and the commitment of a good parent is to be always vigilant to the opportunity to work with the child on the next lesson.

Another important moment of opportunity is what the worlds of business and politics call the "honeymoon period." Most relationships—whether business or personal—start out with a warm period of mutual acceptance. Take the best possible advantage of this initial receptive climate. Quickly choose a course of action with which you can live, then act boldly to put it in place. Take decisive action when a candid but fickle world is willing to give you the short-term benefit of the doubt.

People think that ideas, usually theirs, are the key variable for success. But the right idea at the wrong time gets you nothing but headaches. I will also tell you that if you wait until all the objections to an idea have been addressed and dismissed, the idea will have lost most of its power to help you. During the process of overcoming the arguments against an idea, many more people hear about the idea and become persuaded. And they will go out and start implementing it without you. There's a certain excitement and "jazzed" feeling that comes from delivering an idea. Let the ideas flow when the energy is right for them. Use this excitement or you will lose it.

The need to act quickly on an idea or concept is called urgency. Something can be very important, like the country's need to reduce reliance on foreign fossil fuel. Or it can be urgent, like your car is low on gas. The latter demands immediate attention; the other should be the focus of a great deal of attention in the future or dire things will occur.

It's said that the urgent is seldom important, and the important is seldom urgent. If we don't get gas for the car today, nothing earth shattering will take place. And if we take absolutely no steps toward easing our reliance on foreign fuel today, it's just another day—but the future effects of our non-action may be truly earth shattering.

We need to break down the important things into bite-sized tasks and do some of them each day. When we do, great things will happen. Don't let yourself become so obsessed with your urgent demands that you miss what is truly important. Carve up what is important and dish out slices of it every day.

Here's what we learn from the way the best companies operate: Do as much as you can of the things with important long-term consequences. Do as little as you can of the things that make urgent, short-term demands on your time. In this way, a little of what's important becomes a reality every day. The urgent craziness tends to slip away, leaving room for what will really make a difference in your life. You'll feel better about yourself, because you are using your most important resource—time—to do something that is worthwhile for yourself and your world.

Everything has a gestation period, and it cannot be lengthened or shortened. People try, of course. You may have heard the old question, "If one mother can have a baby in nine months, can nine mothers have a baby in one month?" Maybe trying new and more efficient ways of doing things is good, but for planning purposes, you'd better count on things taking the amount of time that things usually take—which is usually longer than most people think. There are reference tables for predicting solar eclipses, but not for how long you will need to complete the tasks of your life.

People and companies have succeeded in making productivity improvements, cutting the amount of time it takes to do tasks. That's what led to the Industrial Age years ago and to the Information

Revolution we're going through right now. But breakthroughs aren't predictable. They tend to come in fits and starts. Huge gains in productivity are a noble goal, but one shouldn't count on getting nine babies out this month.

Just as each baby and each corporate project has a timeline, each of us has an inherent timetable of development. Parents learn that children go through phases of development at their own pace, and for each child the pattern is one of a kind. Companies are like that, too, which is why each business must be managed using different measurement standards. Your life goals will also have their own unique schedules. Respect them. Use them to your advantage. When you do, time will no longer be an enemy against which you race. Instead, time will become an asset that works for you.

⌁

SIMPLIFYING

Successful businesses simplify complex processes for easy understanding. You, too, need to make things as simple as possible.

Simplicity is an under-appreciated asset. For the most part, however, what is clear and straightforward we retain for future use. If something is too complex for us to grasp or too complicated to do, we tend to pass it by. It has no handles, so it's hard to pick it up and use it. The words "simply brilliant" work well together; simplicity and the light of understanding go hand-in-hand. You have to spoon-feed information to people and take on bite-sized projects for yourself; more than a mouthful is too much to chew.

Unfortunately, though, very few things are more complicated than trying to keep things simple. For the most part, we should use the easiest solution and the lowest level of technology for each problem. The more high-falutin' and ethereal our plan, the greater the chance to screw it up. Our goal must be to win the game, not impress people with the intricacies of our playbook. Simplicity wins the game.

Werner von Braun, the father of modern rocketry, worked for a while at NASA. While there, he was overheard to say, "We can lick gravity, but sometimes the paperwork is overwhelming." He was talking about the need to simplify an effort and not get stuck in the impediments around it. Being a rocket scientist is a complex job, but piercing the atmosphere shouldn't be a cinch compared to piercing red tape.

We too tend to get so bogged down in the "way it is done around here" that we fail to produce results. The better companies set out to simplify their operations so that every person can participate fully in achieving the goals. At the personal level, the more simple our goals, the more apt we are to reach them. By the same token, the more simple our schedules, the more we can accomplish in a day. We're more likely to do a few simple things well than we are to excel at a great many complicated endeavors. Resist the fallacy that says our importance depends on the level of complications in our lives. Simplicity produces excellence.

For each of your roles, keep asking yourself, "What are the basics here?" Then do those things extremely well. That's how good businesses operate, and we should apply this lesson to our various roles as parent, spouse, friend, and employee. Break down each role's expectations to the simplest level. Be dependable; do first things first.

One of the most important basics is to make sure you're not causing your own problems. As doctors would say, "First, do no harm."

Make sure you don't put weapons in the hands of the enemy, and understand that before you can win the war, you must first not lose it. If you want to lose weight, for example, don't make a habit of keeping lots of sweets in the house. If you want to become closer to your spouse, don't expect that to happen if you make a habit of working every evening and weekend. Don't sabotage your own efforts.

Give yourself permission to constantly analyze the environment, be your own best critic, send up trial balloons, and act on the feedback. All too often we ignore our roles' most rudimentary requirements. To prevent this, we have to know each role's core value. For example, the Disney company understands they must keep an amusement park clean, freshly appointed, and filled with smiling attendants.

Why do other companies fail at this basic task? Because management gets bored. They want to do something new and splashy. So they put all their attention into a new roller coaster or a scary flip-over-thingy—and they neglect to inspire the employees to keep the place clean and wear a smile.

We individuals also suffer from this management problem, when we don't do the very basic things we know we should. Life's most essential requirements are pretty simple: floss, exercise, pray, work hard, read positive literature, hug your children, show your spouse your love, call your mom.

We'd often prefer to focus on more complicated and showy routines, but a lifetime of doing the basics each day serves us well indeed. Failing to develop and maintain these habits puts us in an unhappy state and erodes our

> OUR LIFE IS FRITTERED AWAY BY DETAIL. . . . SIMPLIFY, SIMPLIFY, SIMPLIFY.
> —HENRY DAVID THOREAU

confidence in reaching and enjoying success. We need to list our basics and divide them into bite-sized chunks; and then we need to form the personal habit of doing them every single day whether we want to or not.

You'll be more effective if you simplify and distill your messages to others as well. This means that you first boil down your objectives. Make your own goals clear to yourself. Don't try to impress yourself with lots of words! When people asked Jesus to sum up the law, he winnowed it all down to two commandments: "Love the Lord your God with all your heart, with all your soul, and with all your mind . . . and love your neighbor as yourself." The commandments are simple, yet on them "hang all the law and the prophets" (Matthew 22:37-40).

Complexity is highly overrated in our society. The sign of true genius is the ability to cut through all the puff-paste and make things simple and clear. In reality, the premium in life has always gone to those who could lay a message out plainly enough for others to absorb. If you have a friend going through a divorce, you don't have to become an expert on psychotherapy to be of help. Keep it simple. Just being there to listen or help with chores or watch the kids is counseling enough. It's the simple, little things that go a long way.

Understanding the details in most endeavors is grossly overrated, too. I have friends who feel they'll never be able to use a computer because they don't clearly understand what makes it work. Bunk. Do these same people know exactly how an electric typewriter works? Or the mechanism behind a ballpoint pen? We don't need to study how the humble pencil allows us to write before we start scratching out a symphony.

Don't fall into the trap of trying to understand everything. You can't. It's far more important to understand what you want to do and use the right tools to achieve those goals. Simply trust the thing to work. Learn how to work it, not how it works. Always aim for the simplest approach.

Sometimes when a company reaches its market plateau, the urge is to start up something new, to forget the company's strengths. That's a mistake. On a personal level as well, we complicate our lives needlessly when we abandon the simple skills we've developed, and pursue instead new and difficult ventures. This doesn't mean we should never take on new challenges. But we need to first take care of what we've got.

In other words, test the waters before you leap. Use your creativity to improve your key roles and businesses before you venture far from home. The kitchens of the best French chefs tell the tale; exquisite cuisine is not wrestled from the most tortured techniques. Taste leaps out naturally from doing a few simple things very well.

Down deep, people are not complex, either. They just want what they want and want it now. Find out what that is, be yourself, and connect. It's simple.

Strip away all the activities and obsessions that aren't central to your life's mission. If you can't explain why a hobby, relationship, or pursuit makes sense with the rest of your life, you should quietly give it a little vacation until (if ever) its worth becomes clear to you again.

Often we praise the people who come up with the complicated scheme or the "creative" idea, but trod unceremoniously on the person who is earning the profits by carrying the mail. Better companies know that gimmickry and deal making are overrated, and that plain old performance needs to be rewarded.

Customers want results, basic and predictable performance, and the smartest companies in the world deliver that. You should too. Don't be distracted by hot new schemes or techniques you hear about. These contrivances fade. They are not replacements for the basic delivery of results. Don't get trapped into overanalyzing.

Know your true assets—and use them. It's elementary, my dear Watson.

Apply this chapter's key business practices to your own life:

- *First, take inventory in the virtual warehouse of your life. What talents, advantages, and resources do you possess? Write them all down.*

- *Did you include the goodwill of others in your list? How can you maximize your relationships to bring the most benefit both to you and to others?*

- *Determine if you have been seeking out new enterprises while neglecting the assets you already possess. Is there a skill or resource in your life you have failed to develop?*

- *Do you see time as an asset? If not, how can you change your attitude and behavior to make time a resource?*

- *What practical steps could you take to simplify your life? Remember, start small—and simple!*

Six

PLAY TO YOUR STRENGTHS, AND YOU'LL WORK TOWARD CONTENTMENT

Evaluate the role you play best—and go do it!

Both business firms and people are hodgepodges of strengths and weaknesses. No matter how strong they get, they'll always have weaknesses. And regardless of how far they degenerate, the germs of strength still live on. We're stuck (or blessed) with both. Understanding that, the trick seems to be simply getting out of the way of our weaknesses—and then finding ways for our strengths to thrive.

WATER THE FLOWERS, NOT THE WEEDS.
—GISELE RICHARDSON

Empower your strengths and focus on what you can do. Realistically evaluate what you do best and make it your priority. Don't waste time patching up your weak points. Nobody cares what you can't do. Just quietly isolate your weaknesses and systematically render them impotent. Discipline yourself to act on your strengths; use them to benefit others. People interact with you because of your ability to deliver the value created by your strengths. They want and need you to be strong so they can continue to be satisfied. Whether we're speaking of businesses or people, power is firmly rooted in doing some things very well. Make sure people can rely on you to deliver the goods. Leverage your competence adroitly into the lives of others, and, by comparison, your weaknesses will seem puny. Successful corporations do it, and so can you.

<hr />

PLAYING TO YOUR STRENGTHS

Businesses experience success when they determine where their strengths lie and emphasize them. You, too, should identify and play to your strengths.

Beware of the person who, when asked for his strengths, replies, "I am interested in photography." That's not a strength, it's a form of entertainment. A very ugly and charmless man may be interested in the ladies. That doesn't mean he can accomplish anything notable in this area.

Do not try to make your interests serve as the foundation of your vocation. Instead, go with your skills. See if you can find an interesting application for them. Chances are, these will also be your most satisfying and productive activities. If you look at your circle of friends or associates, you'll see how miscast many of them are for what they do. They could be doing something that better suits them and be far more productive and happy. Don't let your passing interests—the ones that come and go, and have little basis in your skills—steer you into an equally unproductive role. Save those fleeting interests for rainy days or snowy nights.

You can't just go and be successful. You have to do what you're good at doing. Doing anything else will be too much work for too little reward. From business we learn that doing what you're good at will be the most rewarding course. It will be personally pleasurable and most highly productive. Find your skills, and you'll also find your joy. The payoffs will be there to reinforce your choice.

The idea is to develop such ponderous strengths that your weaknesses will be overwhelmed and made inconsequential. Don't work on weaknesses. Fixing all of them, even if this were ever possible, would take a lifetime and wear you out. Just keep your foibles out of the way. Life's too short to go up against odds when you don't have to. Work with what you have, not with what you don't have.

You've seen the poster: "If life gives you a lemon, make lemonade." Don't believe it! If you're a lemon at this or that, don't continue making lemonade one more minute. Find out what you're a peach at doing. Refuse to make the best of a bad situation on a long-term basis.

Remember, something is a strength only if others are willing to trade something of value for it. You may be a whiz at making chains out of paperclips, but your skill will do you little good if there's no demand for paperclip chains. You might do better if you applied your manual dexterity to produce some other more valued product.

To seek and sustain a competitive advantage, you really do need

"START RIGHT WHERE YOU ARE. DISTANT FIELDS ALWAYS LOOK GREENER, BUT OPPORTUNITY LIES RIGHT WHERE YOU ARE. TAKE ADVANTAGE OF EVERY OPPORTUNITY OF SERVICE."

—ROBERT COLLIER

to do something special. And like it or not, it is just too hard to be special at something you're not good at doing. You have to compete with the most powerful tools you have. And a Harvard credential may turn out to be no strength at all in a highly competitive arena.

To be a strength, a characteristic must also serve some positive good over the long haul. You may have some passive traits you consider to be strengths—like you may not annoy anyone or you may have a "low maintenance" personality. But these half-baked qualities are not going to improve your competitive position. They may be merely the bland outcomes of failing to commit to one course of action over another. With such characteristics, you may get invited to some neighborhood parties, but you'll never go as guest of honor.

The world is full of average performers doing average jobs at satisfying an average need. But you do not have to operate in that way. You need to focus on doing at least one of the things you do very well. If you do a great job at that one thing, the rewards will allow you to hire someone else to do all of the rest. After all, who really cares if Reggie Jackson can play the fiddle? Who cares if Barbara Walters can fish? Who cared if Malcolm Forbes could fiddle *or* fish? Each of these people had a specific and altogether productive core competence. Around that core he or she built a lifetime of rewards.

Having gained an understanding of this, you can see yourself clearly enough to organize your life strategies around your strengths and weaknesses. You are still you. You are just smarter.

Once you have determined your strengths, go on to make one more step: don't just build on the strengths you have, but experiment in a low-risk way with new behaviors, emerging talents, and undeveloped interests to see if you can uncover some new complementary strength. Be careful, though, about jumping headlong into new interests. The grass does look greener, and a new "hobby" can offer an escape from old responsibilities. If you need recreation, that's fine as long as you don't confuse it with your quest for success. A new interest may or may not be well-coordinated with a skill you already have. Before you invest too heavily in that green grass on the other side of the fence, be sure it will not decrease the property value of the land you already own. Your roles (businesses) have to be at least coordinated with one another.

We get all mixed up about this strength and weakness stuff because when we were kids, our teachers always drilled us on the things at which we were deficient. No good at math? Here came the flash cards. Lousy at oral communications? Up front, you, and tell us about the spots on leopards.

Well, you've grown up now and if you aren't Euclid or Schweitzer, no one cares. You are, however, expected by now to have discovered something you can do well and focused that well-doing for the well-being of society. Remember the world benefits by your success.

CREATING OPTIMAL CONDITIONS

Successful companies do business where they know they will experience the optimum conditions for success. You, too, should create the conditions in your life that will allow your personal strengths to thrive.

There are at least three ways to become strong. One is to shore up your weaknesses. This is largely a waste of time, unless a particular manageable weakness limits your strengths in that area. Another tactic is to improve your strengths, and this has proven to be a good solid approach. But your third choice is the best: you can figure out where your strengths are particularly welcomed, and go there! This is the approach businesses take, and it is the one which is by far the easiest, most natural, and most dramatically fruitful. Very few people, however, take this road. It doesn't occur to them that it even was an option.

Stop banging your head against the wall. Go operate where you're appreciated. Think about who you are and how you come across. Who needs people like that? Find turf where the people will love you—hitchhike there if necessary. Finding your niche is much easier and more rewarding than going through the frustration of trying to improve yourself for an environment that has no appreciation for what you have to offer.

"Blossom where you are planted" may be wise advice in some circumstances. But here's better advice: If the ground is infertile for the kind of seed you have to plant, *move!* Get into an environment that rewards your particular portfolio of attributes. Few people get prizes for hanging in there. Don't wait passively for life to bring about more favorable conditions. Take the initiative. Make decisions that will create the environment where your talents can best be utilized.

Do you ask yourself, "When are they ever going to recognize me?" "When is the boss going to realize that I am the answer to her problems?" If you have to ask, the answer is *never*.

To be recognized, you have to proactively excel. If you are in an environment that has not set you up to use the attributes at which you excel, no one will ever see what your potentials are. Those around you will never give you a break. They will never recognize you. How can they? You are not using the skills and talents by which you hope to be recognized. Bosses, customers, and the world in general only promote or reward people who are performing admirably in their current situation. It will be much harder for you to shine if you're not in a position that conceals your talents and covers your strengths.

If you are a numbers person stuck in the mailroom, it's likely the powers that be won't think of you when they go to fill that job you want in the accounting department because you're not exhibiting the skills necessary for accountants—you don't have the opportunity. What's worse, because you are operating in a situation that is not using your strengths, you are having to throw considerable hard work, discipline, guts, determination, and fortitude into a job that would be a breeze for anyone better suited for the work. You end up looking like the job is killing you; your performance, though it may be exemplary, looks hard won; you are wasting your time; and you are missing out on all of the opportunities to operate more skill-fully from a position of strength. Remember, people get promoted who make their job look easy.

Don't take jobs or attack opportunities for which you lack the necessary skills. The strategy of "getting in," doing an adequate job, and finding the right spot later, is essentially flawed. Because you're no good at what they've already given you, you're not going to get promoted to something else. Unfortunately, the fact that the two positions are vastly different has nothing to do with it. Your year-end performance appraisal still may say you're average. So, when a job opens up, they hire outside the company. Believe me, what looks like a stepping-stone to opportunity will turn out to be a millstone around your neck.

By your agreement to accept a situation outside your core competence, you have neutralized your strengths and congealed an image of yourself in an environment that will institutionalize your mediocrity. Unless you operate on your strengths, the world will never see you as what you want to be. Companies understand this dilemma, and the best firms never foray into environments where they are not recognized as having a competence to sell.

It's better to say *no* when you are offered a mismatched job. Keep looking for a position that requires work you are good at doing. In a hurry to start work, you say? Forget it. You can eat beans and macaroni for a while longer. Half of the hangdog faces in America today can be traced to someone who felt an economic need to take that first, second, or third job—whatever it was—just to feed the kids, pay the rent, or whatever.

You want to excel. Don't sell out. Hold out for an opportunity that draws out your strengths and gives them flesh. If you don't, you'll spend your life frustrated, angrily waiting for people to discover your skills, and they never will. They can't. You're not showing them.

A business doesn't go out to do something it's average at doing in the hopes that customers will recognize in its mediocrity the gleam of talent. Businesses take their best shot the first time, every time. It may be forced to settle for a while, but it won't for long. And neither should you.

Strengths emerge specifically in certain circumstances. For instance, crisis tends to smoke out strengths in people. History shows us this time and time again. People rise to the occasion. In their pre-smoked-out form, their attributes may not have looked like skills. More likely, they may have felt like frustrations. But these same qualities may meet the demands of a new situation, which leads to employment that highlights their strengths.

Don't wait for a crisis. Find the arena where your strengths can do the most good now. If you're terrible at housework, maybe it's time to hire some help so you can focus your energies on the things you do best. If you love mathematics, but you don't have what it takes to get along with adolescents, maybe it's time you stopped teaching high school math and used your skills in the business world. No one is good at everything, and it's not a failure to quit what you're doing and get into something that makes more sense for you.

Finding the right place to use your unique talents is the ultimate success. You'll feel good and accomplish more. And you'll open yourself to all kinds of opportunities you never dreamed of in the days when you were working harder and harder for less and less.

EXPANDING YOUR STRENGTHS

Successful businesses are prepared for the changes various life cycles bring to their appearance of strength. You, too, should fine-tune and expand your strengths over time.

Every business and every person have weaknesses and strengths. The weaknesses happen naturally. Strengths, however, need to be developed. We can't rest on our laurels. We can't assume that our early achievements will carry us through the rest of our lives. For our strengths to flourish, we have to constantly hone them. We have to be committed to a lifetime of fine-tuning our skills.

Music, singing, and dancing are the performing arts at which Barbara Mandrell excels. A worldwide audience knows her capabilities. But her sisters will tell you that Barbara was out of the sack at 5:00 A.M. all through her adolescence giving her "natural" ability a good lot of training and practice. Of course she had talent to work with, but she elevated the threshold of competence by continuing to fine-tune her abilities.

Look for the sustainable competitive advantage. Companies do. Barbara Mandrell did. And understand that the ante—the amount you have to put in just to stay in the game—continues to go up. Examine your strengths in terms of the long haul. How can you continue to demonstrate a particular strength? As others see your success and emulate your steps to achieve it, you may end up with some fleet-footed adversaries playing on your field. You had better think through the likely life cycles of your particular skill and plan how you hope to maintain your edge.

If we list our current skills and weaknesses, then we can consider how both will appear in the years that lie ahead. For example, if being an uncoordinated, bespectacled nerd is a problem for a high school chess champion, will his problems get better or worse once he is out of graduate school? Will his strategic thinking and analytical approach serve him well in the business world? What about his classmate, the basketball star? Does *his* strength have a future? Will his "basketball" body and "rebound" mind-set be of value when he is twenty-eight? We can each benefit from examining our strengths and weaknesses as they will look a decade from now. Will we have what it takes to pull off the success we are planning?

If you're not going to have what it takes, take what you have and do something else with it. Don't feed your resources to something that will do you little good in the years ahead. And if it will take five years for your plan to unfold, the attributes required to achieve that success need to be planted now in order to blossom later.

Encourage yourself to look down the line to see what could grow from your unfolding strengths. Determine the life cycles that lie ahead. Decide how to fine-tune today's strengths to meet tomorrow's needs. You have much more power to shape the future than you think.

People are amazingly impatient. They get all wadded up in the ambition of the moment. When today's efforts fail, they give up. But if you can overcome the frustration that comes from trying to do too much too soon too well, you will see that you can virtually always accomplish more than you had ever imagined over the long haul.

One way to operate successfully over time includes developing your strengths so that they are "transplantable." Obviously, you should focus on what you're doing, but make sure your skill can be used in other environments should it become expedient to move it there quickly. Be sure your strengths have broad enough applications so that they can be used in even bigger ways in some other place. You never know when your support environment will disintegrate, and you'll need to keep going despite the loss of your familiar circumstances. Your strengths will carry you through, but only if you have managed to keep them transferable.

For instance, you may know a great deal about how to interact with the computer system and the systems people on your job. This means you know a great deal about interacting with the computer systems and the people who use them at other companies as well. Your skill is relevant to other situations should it become necessary or otherwise advisable to move. By the same token, in your personal life, you may feel your teenage children no longer need the parenting skills you developed when they were toddlers. While it's true your kids don't need you to play peek-a-boo or horsy with them anymore, your parenting skills may not be as obsolete as they appear at first glance. A sense of humor, commitment, and resolve can be as useful now that your children are adolescents as those strengths were when your kids were preschoolers.

As time passes, you need to be willing and able to apply your skills in new and unique ways. People tend to feel that if they've done their job well once, they'll be successful forever. But that's not realistic. Most roles, most careers, and most companies won't last as long as you will.

So don't only become good at cutting your daughter's hair; learn how to cut all hair. Your daughter may want to change her hairstyle (maybe frequently). If your strengths are designed and developed to do only the specific tasks on which you currently labor, you'll only be good at that one task. Broaden the scope. Yes, continue to focus on being the world's best at your work, but widen your eyes to see the context in which that job is done. Be sure your strengths also satisfy related needs—should you one day need them to do so.

> YESTERDAY'S ANSWER HAS NOTHING TO DO WITH TODAY'S PROBLEM.
> —BILL GATES

Don't expect your strengths to be automatically transferable. You'll have to work hard to make that happen. Endeavor to find out how the rest of the world uses this strength you have. Try out some of what works for the rest of the world in your own little corner of it, and you'll find your strength improving.

~≋~

LIVING WITH YOUR FLAWS

Successful businesses find ways to compensate for their weaknesses. You, too, should learn to live with your personal flaws.

Ninety percent of your activity ought to focus on identifying and fortifying your strengths. That leaves the other ten percent for your weaknesses. You need to know your limitations just like you need to know those of your car before you head over the mountains. Don't fret; just get the belts checked and put in the oil. Deal defensively with your weaknesses, while you're aggressively offensive with your strengths.

Accept your faults. Come to terms with them. Don't beat yourself up over your imperfections. Just don't put yourself in a position where you have to rely on your weaknesses instead of your strengths. Your goal instead is to operate in environments where your problem areas won't matter. You don't want to spend time, effort, or energy battling them, so organize around them. Remember, just check the belts, put in the oil, no big deal. Render your weaknesses impotent, so your strengths can flourish.

Weaknesses don't actually weaken you unless they are apparent, demonstrated, operative, or acted out. It's only a weakness if it limits a strength. It's only a weakness if it's a competitive disadvantage. Poets do not need a working knowledge of cost accounting. Accountants do not need to be basketball pros. I do not need hair on the top of my head for the life I lead.

Can't carry a tune in a bucket? Don't join the choir—no matter how much pressure is exerted. Go ahead and be a part of their group if you must—but mail their announcements for them, do their paperwork for them, draw up posters for them. Just don't let them talk you into singing.

Think how many times you've operated in a situation that you knew wasn't right for you. You settled because you felt you "ought to." Don't. If you do, you won't be doing anyone any favors, least of all yourself.

Once again, the issue of integrity becomes apparent. You don't hide the fact that you're not a whiz at math; you just don't interview for positions that require it in any salient way. You tell the truth and nothing but the truth. But you do not self-incriminate. You don't have to. You possess good, worthwhile talents that deserve a chance to grow. Don't hinder them by throwing them into an environment that forces them to play second fiddle to a weakness.

This is not to say that you can ever ignore your weaknesses altogether. They will be with you always. Never forget that. Your knowledge of your entire self, limitations and all, must continue to grow. And some day, circumstances may be such that what once looked like a weakness is now exactly what's needed to save the day. Be open to the possibilities.

Learn the boundaries of your strengths as well. If you are the creative director, stop when your expertise ends. Don't try to put the concept into production. Let the people in the plant do that. Go do the next brainstorm. Companies have learned this time and time again. The business firm passes the project from R&D to production once the creative part of it is complete. Such practice, altogether commonplace in industry, enables both departments to use what they're good at doing, and lets each, in turn, get psyched up for the next one.

Strengths are very specific. They have limited application, while weaknesses tend to be far more common. The key to success is to leverage off our strengths, whether we're a company or an individual. Why companies, organizations, and humans in general insist on operating in their spheres of weakness is beyond my comprehension. Businesses are forced to learn quickly to use their strengths, or they are no longer in business. Unfortunately, this self-destructive behavior continues unchecked in many individuals.

Business has learned that it can't make a quick buck in a field it doesn't know, or isn't likely to master. Many people, however, desperate for a new CD system, take their first job in an area they don't like, in which they won't excel, with the pathetic notion that they can go get a job that they're "good at" later. They make enough to buy the CD system, but they are miserable forty hours a week.

In the meantime, the smart ones, the excited ones, the devoted ones, tramp the pavement to get a start-up job in a field they know they're equipped and configured to handle. They have already begun the process of assimilating the techniques that will nourish and complement their naked, uninformed strengths.

When you work, your employer is paying you for your strengths. You are not paid for your weaknesses. In your personal life as well, your limitations should be neither seen nor heard. Keep them as quiet as you can. Be sure they are not eking energy away from your strengths.

Don't depend on your mother, your best friend, or even your spouse to tell you what your weaknesses and strengths are. Mothers, friends, and society as a whole focus on easy rewards. For instance, medical and legal careers are obvious favorites, since their monetary awards are so apparent. But our weaknesses cannot be erased simply by encouragement, love, and hard work. It's not that simple. No matter how lucrative a profession, we're unlikely to excel at it if it lies within the realm of our weaknesses rather than our strengths.

The world is always amazed when people deviate from the structured paths to success and pursue instead what they are good at. They're the ones who win the Nobel Prize in literature, who do groundbreaking work in research, who add something truly new to our world. They're also the ones who are fulfilled and excited by their lives. It happens so infrequently that it is truly a joy to see unfold.

Why continue to fumble through life while you strive to keep up in an area you'll never master? Who wants to be incompetent? Good things happen to those who work consistently with their core of competencies.

When companies are in trouble, they protect their business core, while they divest themselves of whatever could weaken them. You too should do whatever it takes to protect your talents. Before Donald Rumsfeld became secretary of defense for the administration of George W. Bush, he was a successful executive who took over the troubled G. D. Searle company. To save the business, he had to sell off 1,100 dramatically successful Pearl Vision Centers in order to shore up the company's historical base business in drugs. He protected, developed, and leveraged the strengths of the core. We sometimes call this core the Mother Lode, because in its veins flow the golden hope of survival. In Rumsfeld's case, his sacrifice paid off nicely. He then focused the Searle empire's strengths in order to magnify them. As a result, he transformed the ailing company into a powerhouse.

❦

USING YOUR STRENGTHS FOR GOOD

Successful companies become powerful to the extent that they fill a bona fide need. People possess true power as well when they use their strengths to benefit the world.

People think of Stalin or Attila the Hun when they think of power. The power those guys wielded was based on intimidation and physical threat. It's the sort of strength that only survives through the sacrifices of the downtrodden. It has no life-sustaining attributes. One slip, and it's gone.

But the power of Beethoven and Shakespeare is much greater than that of any dictator or conqueror. This sort of power is not evil. It means you have people who choose to be involved with you. It's a public trust.

Creative power is uplifting. It energizes society. For example, good authors encourage us to be all we were meant to be. We surrender our eyes and brains to the writer and invite her to treat us with her inspiration. Once satisfied, this kind of power sustains itself, feeds on successes, and encourages us to become far more. We voluntarily listen and we go back for more. That's good power.

All of the good that's been done in the world has happened because the most worthwhile of us humans understood and responsibly used their competencies to improve the world. We flock to such people because we trust and respect them to deliver that which is in our continued best interest. We ask them to be stewards of our future.

For individuals, power is achieved in much the same way as it is achieved by business: You develop a practical solution to a need no one else has taken the time or expended the energy to see and satisfy . . . People start depending on you to fill that need, and all of a sudden, your influence, worth, and, yes, your power increase.

Inconspicuously volunteer. Wipe up the unfinished and dragging jobs others are reluctant to complete. Pick up the overflow work of someone who will gladly let you "try" to do it on a temporary basis. Do not step on toes or pick jobs obviously in the fighting territory of someone else. Invent meaningful things that would be of value for you to continue. Create "new products." Be constantly vigilant. Repeat this process and eventually your job description bears only the slightest resemblance to your behavior. (Which is what people remember, anyway.) You will have gained power and influence. People start coming to you. Power is a spin-off benefit others bestow on you because you took the initiative to leverage your strengths to do something extremely useful for them.

Don't go out to take power from other people. Create your own by spending your energy on things people value. They in turn will deliver power back to you.

Ok . . . a test. Why did the mafia become powerful in this country? No, it's not because of the machine guns in the violin cases. It was because they filled a need no one else was willing or able to address: supplying liquor during Prohibition. They took the heat and thereby protected their customers.

I'm not recommending that you use the mafia as a universal role model. But they can teach us well in this area. In order to maintain or grow their power, firms—and people—must manage their transactions in such a way as to ensure that the customer is satisfied and definitely wants to come back. If that influence (power) over the customer is ever harmed, the fortunes of the company are in serious jeopardy.

It's like a parent dealing with a teenager. If the parent is overbearing and tries to force the teenager to behave a certain way or be involved in certain activities that don't match his personality, he will rebel, and possibly become self-destructive. However, if the parent listens to the teenager to see what he likes and encourages the good behavior with love and acceptance, the teenager will, most likely, respond positively.

Power is the by-product of developing and delivering your strengths in such a way as to gratify the recipient. Power is specific, not universal. Power, like its predecessor, strength, should only be used in the appropriate environment. As a by-product, power and influence can only be effectively used in circumstances that value it. For instance, our salaries are the by-product of the value we deliver to our employers.

The American greenback dollars you receive in a paycheck in Hoboken, however, won't necessarily be recognized as having value in Jakarta. Some translation must occur. And, it may be that your power could never be sufficiently repackaged to carry any weight in Indonesia. Understand the local application of power. It is not universal. The things that influence one group of people may have no effect over another group. The power you possess in one role is not automatically transferable to another role.

But for whatever role in which you function, ask yourself: "What do I want my power to accomplish?" The answer must be something that will benefit your customers—your friends and family—or your power will never take hold. Power is like money. You had better spend it on things that will keep your customers coming back. As long as you understand that "power seeking" is seldom successful, you can begin to become the success you envision.

You do not gain or lose power directly. It happens only through other people who will act to empower or diminish you. Power is a gift given to you in exchange for the gifts you offer the world. While you cannot create power all on your own, without interaction with others, the list on the next page spells out power's foundation in your life.

The old image of gaining

> I USE THE BUSINESS TO MAKE GREAT PEOPLE. I DON'T USE PEOPLE TO MAKE A GREAT BUSINESS.
> —RALPH STAYER

POWER & INFLUENCE

COMES FROM:	IS LOST BY:
Being truthful	Being deceitful
Having integrity	Having poor ethics
Having patience	Being impatient
Being competent	Blundering
Seeing the big picture	Being narrowly focused
Providing inspiration	Tearing others down
Being part of something	Being egocentric
Taking initiative	Doing only what is expected
Being committed	Being scatter-brained
Being prepared	Not being prepared
Being a contributor	Being a consumer
Relying on others	Not asking for help
Networking	Isolating yourself
Being a good sport	Winning at all costs
Giving others credit	Being conceited
Simplifying things	Complicating things
Doing favors for people	Being high maintenence
Following up	Not coming through
Taking inventory of yourself	Not knowing your strengths and weaknesses
Communicating clearly	Confusing others
Fair-mindedness	Being bloodthirsty
Caring for others	Being indifferent
Serving others	Being selfish
Being passionate	Being obsessed
Persistence	Giving up

power by beating people over the head has long since failed. Beating people wears them out and makes them powerless to do what we want anyway. Besides, they'll never voluntarily cooperate with us again. Instead, we become greater by using our strengths to do things that will help people. They recognize the help and return rewards that empower us. Don't use your strengths to control others; use those strengths instead to enrich the world.

⚬❦⚬

GETTING ON THE BALL

Successful companies don't wait to utilize every potential. As an individual, you also should use your skills now.

An insidious and terrible trap attaches itself to having talent. It's the "I'll use it tomorrow" trap. It's similar to the alcoholic trap— "I can quit tomorrow"—and it's just as intoxicating. Go out there now and do something that uses these talents. Talent alone will not deliver your dreams.

What if Barbara Mandrell hadn't gotten up at 5:00 A.M.? Don't save up your talent for some later moment. That would be counting on an untested potential, and it's too big a risk for any sane management to take. If companies don't do it that way, neither should you.

Use those talents, now. Refine them. Discipline yourself to work on improving them, not only for when you might need them tomorrow, but for right now. You might as well start enjoying the rewards of life.

We all have heard the stories about the woman who lifted the car to get her child out of the wreckage. Why wait for a crisis to show your strength? Start lifting today. You'll be amazed at the Herculean proportions your strengths will take. And you never know, having used and encouraged your strength, you may be able to lift a *bus* if you ever need to, and one day our kids will all be telling stories about *you*.

Apply this chapter's key points to your own life:

LIST YOUR TOP FIVE STRENGTHS

- *What conditions do your strengths need to flourish? What actions do you need to take to create those conditions?*

- *How can you let go of a need for perfection—and instead focus on being better at what you do than those around you?*

- *Is there a skill in your life that you have postponed using? How can you begin using that strength today?*

- *How will upcoming life cycle changes affect your strengths? Will you be able to transfer your skills to new situations? How?*

LIST YOUR FIVE MAIN WEAKNESSES

- *How can you work around these flaws? How can you keep them from getting in the way of your strengths?*

- *How can you use your strengths to limit your weaknesses?*

Seven

IF YOU JUST STICK YOUR TOE IN THE WATER, YOU'LL MISS THE BOAT

Take decisive action;
whatever the role, know what to do when.

Analysis is a worthwhile endeavor, and it has its moments. But studying various strategies is a very different behavior from decision making or problem solving. Sometimes you need to take time to figure out what your options, opportunities, and potentials might be. Other times you need to take decisive action. One skill should not be used when another is warranted.

Do not:

- think when you should act

- act when you should first seek out the facts

- make a choice when you should analyze

- analyze when you should be brainstorming

- leap ahead when it's really time to think and ponder

- hesitate when you should leap

The ability to use the right skill at the right time is rare, but also easy to master if given some thought and practice. Make a conscious choice to select the action specifically suited for the job you need to do. Pull a particular skill from your toolbox only when you have a job that requires it. Don't dilly-dally. Act!

~

IDENTIFYING THE PROBLEM

Successful companies first define a problem before they try to solve it. Individuals also need to identify their problems, or they will most likely try to solve the wrong problem.

People have a tendency to make up a solution to the problem before they clearly fix the nature of the problem in their minds. If you have squirrels in your attic, our friends who love animals will want to trap the squirrels and release them miles away. If the owner of the home with squirrels in the attic is an avid hunter, however, his solution will be to shoot the varmints! We tend to use the skills that are most readily available to us to solve our problems. That may work in the short term, but over time, more squirrels will sneak in. The best solution is to seal up the entrances to your attic so squirrels can't get in. You don't have a squirrel problem. You have a holey house problem.

When a problem crops up, I have learned that the very best companies always look first at what has changed. What is different that could have caused the problem to express itself now? What is going on now that didn't go on before this problem reared its ugly head? Linger on this answer because the responses you get to those questions are exactly what you need to know in order to fix it. Don't leap to creating solutions. Follow these steps:

- Define what is wrong (state the problem).

- Look for the cause (what changed just before the problem began).

- Identify your desired results.

Once you have figured out the cause of the problem, then state to yourself (and to those who are going to help you) just what you would like to see instead of the current situation. With a clear view of what is wrong, how it got there, and what you would like to see different, you are finally ready to start brainstorming solutions. Of course, the minute you find the best solution you can, you'll discover that there are problems with your solution. So what? *All* solutions have problems. Find the problems associated with your chosen solution and fix those, too.

Problem solving doesn't need to be a reactionary discipline. You don't have to wait until your car breaks down before fixing it. You should seek out problems proactively; that's called maintenance. This is why America is so great. We prize innovation and the companies that introduce it. We are thrilled because they think of solutions to problems we might otherwise accept. No one needed a DVD player until everyone "needed" one.

As long as we are alive, we will have problems. While they're a downer at first, when we start to peel away the layers and get to the core of the issues, we see we have many tools for solving the problems.

MAKING A PLAN

A successful company defines the appropriate business practice for each situation. You, too, should make a plan to determine the right skill at the right time.

If you tell your boy that you are going to "help him" build a doghouse on Saturday, he'll probably go to bed Friday night with a hammer next to his pillow and wake up early the next morning ready to start swinging it. The thought may bring a smile to your face, but such behavior is not so cute when exhibited by an adult. Young and old alike, we all tend to jump into things without first thinking, researching, deciding, and solving as though activity has merit of its own accord. We'd proceed more efficiently if we first determined which skill is needed when.

How many times in your life has someone asked you how you *think* you spell a word? Well, if you don't *know*, no thinking is required. We have spell-check programs and dictionaries. Use them. Do your research! Thinking is exactly the wrong skill to use when it's time to find out how to spell something or to answer a question like, "Who was the first secretary of state?" You can think all night and you won't be one iota closer to an answer. Look up the things that need to be researched.

Have you ever encountered a person who wanted to "decide" what would happen if two chemicals are mixed together? This is another form of confusion that happens all the time. There is no "deciding" involved. You could decide ten different things and none of them would have any impact on the outcome. What you have is a problem. The process on which to rely in this case is problem-solving behavior, which is different from decision making in almost every particular. To solve a problem, you need to have a plan: define the problem, set up a scientific method to isolate a solution, and test variables until a conclusion is reached.

Way back in medieval England, King John showed us that we waste time if we employ techniques that have no import. He had his footmen carry his throne down to the sea and commanded the tides not to touch his cloak. When he was wet up to his bum, the footmen came and fished him out, thereby demonstrating the limits of royal authority. The king knew that nature didn't follow his plan just as he knew that a decree "for the birds" was worthless. John knew there were times thinking and acting could make a difference, and there were times when it did not.

When making a plan some people are confused about when to analyze and when to act. I remember my father telling me about an engineer he worked with who got this one wrong. "If we had a wall falling down, and I needed him to simply grab a two-by-four to shore it up, this man would run back to the office to design the perfect solution. In the meantime, the wall would crumble." Analysis is a wonderful thing. But when the dike springs a leak, every little Dutch boy knows to stick his finger into it. Action is sometimes required before the formation of a fact-finding committee.

In all of this, the key is to pause for a split second to see if you can figure out what kind of circumstance is being presented to you. Is it time to solve a problem? Decide something? Look something up? Suspend judgment? In that instant, clarity will come, but you must provide yourself that pause. You need to either research, choose between alternatives, figure out a puzzle, or consciously elect not to act at this juncture. Be careful about which you choose. Make acting and thinking productive by selecting the right tool to use in each circumstance.

If you are having trouble balancing your family budget, you have a decision to make. Will you continue to operate in the red, find a new job, or cut back? If you decide to find a new job, you are temporarily finished with decisions and need to do some research.

Once you come up with sufficient information, it's time to decide things again. You have narrowed your choices to three companies, and now you have a problem to solve. How will you convince a boss in one of these companies to hire you? You have nothing left to research. You have no other decisions to make. You have a problem to solve: how to get them to hire you.

Many people think it's time to make a decision when really it's time to seek information. They think it's decision time just because they've come to a fork in the road. No, first you have to find out everything you can about where each road leads. Yes, there is a choice to be made, but rushing to make it is highly counterproductive if what you really need is analysis, research, or information. When you confront a situation, try to group it into one of these categories:

1. *Research.* When you really don't have enough information, and you have time to collect data.

2. *Decision making.* When you have sufficient knowledge, including the positive or negative consequences of deciding.

3. *Problem solving.* When the information level is okay, and there's no decision to make, but there's still a riddle to pursue.

4. *Suspending judgment.* When you decide not to decide

because there is no imminent consequence (positive or negative) of withholding a decision now.

All these tools are perfectly legitimate and warranted in different situations. When in doubt as to which action to take, I recommend that you take a stand to the right of foot dragging, and make sure you have a plan.

Decision making

Successful businesses have procedures for determining how and when to make decisions. You, too, can develop and follow real-life procedures that will help you with the decision-making process.

The best model I know for structured decision making is the methodology embedded in the *Places Rated Almanac*. Local variables from weather and recreation to education and tax rates are first scaled in importance. Then various cities are rated against the variables. If a low cost of living is your number one factor in choosing a city, you will end up someplace very different than you would if living next to the ocean is number one. If you agree with the process, you will agree with the outcome of the process. Grab a copy of this book. It can be a guide for your decision making whether you are selecting a school, deciding where to take the family vacation, or laboring over what kind of puppy you should buy.

When selecting which variables are priorities in your life (for instance, "cost of living" or "near an ocean") you are making a decision. When determining whether Kansas City or Los Angeles is a less expensive city, you are looking up facts. Facts are out there, and with the Internet on fire around us, people are bathed in facts.

Before you do anything, simply stop everything. Sit in a quiet place for a short time and answer this question: How will I go about solving this problem? You must commit to following a methodology. If not, your efforts to wrestle down this monster will be random and messy. If you spend just a few moments determining how to solve the problem, the actual resolution of it will be quicker and easier. If you just jump in and begin with no strategy in mind, you will make yourself and everyone else around you crazy. Force yourself to identify the process you plan to employ in solving your problems. If you commit to following a process, you will have a plan to follow. This also allows you to collect feedback about how you are doing. It will help you make a decision.

One day in high school I was hanging out with a friend on the back deck of his house. From it, we could view his whole back yard, in which I noticed a strange curlicue pattern of green grass snaking all around the yard. Some of the grass lush and colorful while the rest was tired and full of weeds. It turns out that at the beginning of spring my friend's mom set off with a push spreader filled with weed killer and fertilizer. She started by aiming at the dandelions; she rolled over the first one, and then aimed for the next one and so on until her tiller was empty. Weeks later, her unique "process" was exposed. It was a hoot.

But isn't that exactly the way life unfolds when we don't have a plan and make decisions ahead of time? We end up with random squiggles that fail to accomplish our intended goal. And once we employ a conscious methodology to solve problems, we won't ever want to go back. The critical imperative is not what to do, but how to determine what to do.

Often we go to "experts" and ask them what we should do. And it is fine to listen to their advice and even to follow it, but the advice we really need to listen to isn't "What should I do?"; it's "How should I approach this?" It's the difference between giving a child a fish and teaching him how to fish. Next time you aren't sure what to do, avoid the temptation to ask a trusted mentor, "What do you think I should do?" Instead, rephrase your request to ask how she or he might help you think through this problem. Doing this helps boil out the thought processes behind the advice. That is the golden egg. When wise advisers start talking about approach, strategy, and process, that's when you shut up and listen.

Every decision will inevitably annoy someone therefore you should only make necessary decisions. If the outcome of a decision doesn't affect you, and you don't care what happens, say so. If you do care, say so. But don't meddle. If you don't have a dog in this fight, and see no need to decide, don't decide right now. On the other hand, don't fail to participate in any decision that affects your life. Also, jump in quickly if the decision is reversible, less quickly if it isn't. I recommend erring on the side of action. Most of what we consider decision making is actually making a simple selection from two or more possibilities that will end up just fine, no matter what we choose.

In the presence of a need to decide something, not deciding is almost always the worst thing you can do. If you need to decide, do it promptly and confidently, and back it up with supportive action. In most companies, the stress and strain of decision making is far less wearing than the constant business of not deciding.

Another mistake in decision making is wavering after the fact. There are enough people out there who will second guess you, but one of the surest ways to prove yourself wrong is to fail to support your own decision with words and deeds. When the history of the decision is written, you may look bad if you made the wrong decision, but you will look just as bad if you made the right decision but failed to implement it properly.

The world is full of clowns who are willing to make their opinions known. That isn't decisiveness. A decisive person puts her money and her time on the line. A decisive person pushes hard to execute the decision. Start with what you know. You can never have all the facts, but discern what you can and write that down as a "given." Also, state what you know the answer *isn't*. It's much easier to recognize error than to find truth.

There is one more thing I must tell you about decision making. We've already said that many times there are several correct choices, and your job is to pick one. So try this: In addition to picking the "right answer," see if you can write down the "next right answer." You still go with the first one, but you'll always know of another path you can take that will work also.

This idea of a "second right answer" liberates and invigorates you. It gives you the safety net of an idea you know will also work. You can focus on making the first decision a reality without having to second guess yourself or cover your back. This is a very good thing. Companies do it and call it contingency planning. You should do it, too.

✥

TAKING ACTION

A successful business takes action based on the facts it possesses. You, too, should know when to stop the fact-gathering process and move on to the next step.

Of all the people in the history of the world, few are more famous than Julius Caesar. And why is he famous? Because he made a decision to cross the Rubicon. There were a lot of Roman governors at the time, and Julius was the one from Gaul, the area we now call France. The rule was that governors of Roman provinces were not to approach Rome with their troops. Caesar in particular was under strict orders from the Roman Senate not to cross a river called the Rubicon in Northern Italy. In fact, the senate had relieved him of his responsibilities and ordered him to return to Rome alone. The senators feared Caesar and his growing power.

Caesar didn't think too highly of their idea to abandon his troops and leave himself defenseless at their hands. On January 19, 49 B.C., Caesar made the decision to cross the Rubicon River with his troops. He meant business . . . about himself. The expression, "to cross the Rubicon" has come to mean a bold, decisive, and irreversible step. In this case, it meant the precipitation of a civil war that eventually led to Caesar ruling the Roman Empire.

> THE FACT IS WE'LL NEVER HAVE ALL THE INFORMATION WE NEED TO MAKE A DECISION— IF WE DID, IT WOULD BE A FOREGONE CONCLUSION, NOT A DECISION.
>
> —DAVID MAHONEY

The business world is replete with lesser-known stories of bravado, street smarts, and guts. It takes all of those attributes and more to run a company. Though thousands of sheets roll off computer printers in an attempt to analyze where the wells should be dug in the North Sea, humans eventually have to pick a spot and start drilling; they have to take action. While scores of analysts plow through reams of marketing data, an actual human manager must eventually select the name for a new cereal. And despite the way Wall Street values a stock, the CEO must ultimately decide whether layoffs are warranted. His own job is at risk when he makes this decision. But only he can make it.

In every case from Caesar to Bill Gates, analysis was needed. You must have as many facts as you can gather before you commit. And a structured approach to fact gathering is critical. But in most cases, with most decisions, you won't have the time to gather all the information you'd like to have. Once you have all the facts you have time to gather, *take action!* This applies to a new product launch, getting married, crossing the Rubicon, or picking a name for a baby.

Almost everything can be fixed or changed or modified or improved later. Most decisions aren't life or death. You don't need *all* the facts. The key is to apply the facts you have to the general direction in which you are headed, and then make the best decisions you can to get closer to the spot where you hope to end up.

This is what companies do. They cannot possibly tell all their employees which type of pencils to buy and which laptops to lease. They would be foolish to prescribe the color of the consumer goods or the price on every item.

What is the Rubicon you need to cross to move into a new phase of leadership in your life? Find it and cross it.

<hr />

BEING CONSISTENT

Successful companies have a plan and make decisions that are consistent with that plan. You, too, should be consistent with the plan for your life.

I've said before that thinking is overrated. We don't have to start at the beginning each time we encounter a problem. It's like using cruise control in your car. If you are sailing down the highway and all is well, let cruise control do its job. But when you see red taillights, step on the brake and take back control. Start thinking. Make decisions. Solve problems. The better companies don't let cruise control run away with their futures. They don't use policy manuals when judgment is required. But they certainly run their diverse organizations "by the book." This liberates them, not constrains them.

McDonald's has become a multibillion-dollar empire based on the delivery of consistent quality. You always know what you are going to get. There are no surprises. McDonald's management certainly does not want their counter people to "experiment" with holding the sliced potatoes in the fryer an extra five seconds. They want folks to go by the book. But if someone on the front lines has a great idea about how to improve the fries, there is a suggestion program with incentives to collect and report those creative ideas. Successful companies like McDonald's have learned to harness creative thinking on one hand and limit it on the other. Both are needed.

Some people may fear that such advice will turn us into slaves to procedure who can never break out of the mold. Wrong. What I am telling you is that thinking is highly overrated and misused; it isn't used when it is really needed.

Shakespeare wrote in iambic pentameter, but his works aren't boring or formulaic. Old Will used great creativity, but he didn't waste it on format. He stuck with the structure and got superlative results.

Companies are great at this. They make it so that every person doesn't have to wake up every morning and decide how to answer the company's phone. When you have a personal strategic plan in place as well, it's easy to decide what to get involved with and what to avoid. You will develop deep commitment to your plans, and you will be able to take actions boldly without fear that they won't make sense in your life. Once you internalize your goals, the way companies tack their mission statements on their cafeteria walls, your decisions will increasingly come from within you. Intuition forms and builds, and it will boil out of all your past experiences, knowledge, and feelings, creating a sense of confidence to deal with the issues of the day. You will remain consistent with your plan and character.

It's not that analysis is bad. It is an absolutely critical tool when used appropriately. But the analysis should never get in the way of action. Your actions should be part of a methodology and your actions should be directed toward your objectives. Analyze your objectives, develop an approach to them, then measure every action against this model. This can be instantaneous.

Companies often are reluctant to do what they know they should do. Managers hate to fire people. They would rather not make people work overtime. No one in the business world likes killing the products that got them this far and replacing them with new ones that are not guaranteed to thrill the public. But they do it; they make the decisions they need to make without betting the ranch. First they compare every potential change against the strategy statement we've talked about. Then they make certain they test their way into things instead of risking the entire enterprise.

When you're acting in line with your personal strategy, or plan, you, too, can move ahead without fear or remorse.

ACTING BETTER

The one business rubric that is tantamount to success is: Get started! On the personal level, as well, you cannot feel your way into acting better; you must act your way into feeling better.

If companies and individuals wait until they feel like going on a diet or cutting deadwood, it's unlikely they will ever begin. When you are buried under too much inventory, you can't afford the carrying costs long enough to feel better about it. You need to start selling it off immediately, and eventually the company (as measured by its financial statements) will start feeling better. If you feel bad because you are portly, you can't wait until you feel better about yourself to start losing your weight. You have to act your way into feeling better by eating responsibly and exercising consistently.

One thing that companies often do better than individuals is deliver bad news. When some bottles of Tylenol were poisoned, the company recalled its product quickly and responsibly. The company came out of the situation smelling like a rose. When there is bad news to deliver, it's best to deliver the news and get it behind you as quickly as possible.

It's a curious twist that the more controversial an issue is, the more frank and direct you must be. We are all built in such a way that we want to waffle on the hard points and try to "soften the blow." This is exactly the wrong reaction. If your company needs to terminate an employee, you will be kind to do it privately, professionally, and with finality. Spinning out strings of hope is the cruelest thing you can do. The same goes with your love life. Do not string the person along. Be bold, be frank, be kind, but be direct. Pussyfooting just means you'll have to have another painful conversation later.

The best companies do not deliver bad news a spoonful at a time. Nothing will make a consumer more angry than if a company fails to come clean about what is going on and how it affects them. Spineless communication has no place in business, nor, I would suggest, in your personal life.

Sure, there are companies that flunk this test. But the best companies enter a novel situation and size it up quickly, act boldly, and communicate frankly to all of the parties involved. These are the successful ones, and the ones that deserve our emulation.

⤳

CHOOSING YOUR BATTLES

Successful companies take on challenges carefully. You, too, should pick your battles wisely.

When you start a war, do so consciously. Attack knowing that you are doing so. Never get sucked into a conflict you haven't anticipated. Understand where the tradeoffs are and choose them. Be sure that you pick the timing for any battle you get in as well. It is as important as the terrain.

Choose the weapons you will use. You have to constantly ask yourself what the best use of your time and energy is. This is the key to resource allocation. Understand that you can compete effectively by competing in ways that change the rules. People tend to see only the objectives that are obvious in the current situation. And we tend to develop our objectives incrementally, saying we want to grow and be bigger and better. The assistant manager wants to be manager; the colonel wants to be general and the cardinal wants to be pope. You probably want to have your boss's job or you want your current company to grow by 10 percent next year. But if you are in the wrong strategic place, it doesn't matter where your growth leads. Focus on determining the right place for yourself and the kinds of things you ought to be doing now. You can't fight tomorrow's battles today.

Don't choose every battle. Study your timing carefully. It is very important to fix the right things at the right time. Choose projects that have a premium payoff at a time that is right for you. When you get involved in a new situation, a new city, a new job, or a new relationship, take note of the things that strike you as being odd. They probably *are* odd, but don't fight them the minute you arrive. As a newcomer you can't show an exaggerated interest in these quirks lest you retard your assimilation into the culture there. Wait till you become a trusted member of the group. When you have gained understanding and influence, pull out your notes and see what initially appeared strange to you.

You'll undoubtedly have received an education since first observing the odd phenomenon. You are probably quite accustomed to it now, too. But you still may understand it to be quite wrong. When you get in a position to do something about it, do something about it.

Go after the easy stuff first. Do what you already know you should do. Don't take on a massive project that will make you buckle under its weight. Don't take on projects that require extensive justification. Figure out the really important things that will produce results quickly and focus on them. If you have a raft of projects that need to be done, select some at the very outset that will produce results and make people feel good about your leadership and themselves. This applies to business—and to a church committee or local parent-teacher association.

You must understand the message you are trying to lay out. If you're trying to send a message, don't fight the people you're sending it to in an effort to convince them to change their minds. Find out what is already in their heads and position your message so they can hear it.

NEVER DOUBT THAT A SMALL GROUP OF THOUGHTFUL COMMITTED PEOPLE CAN CHANGE THE WORLD; INDEED IT IS THE ONLY THING THAT EVER HAS.

—MARGARET MEAD

Choose your battles. Commit where you think you can make a difference. Go with the flow. Anticipate the events that will happen naturally and conspire with the world to be there with a solution to any problems that will result. Commit your resources where they are likely to pay off. Don't knock your head against brick walls. Don't start any fights you cannot win. You have to be able to leave some things alone. Go *around* the competition, not head to head.

A long time ago, I decided that the hairstyles of my kids would not be a hill for me to die on. They have had hairstyles that were as outlandish as anything I could imagine. They had some that made them, in my opinion, less attractive. Some were way too long; some were way too short. Some had parts that were too long and too short at the same time! Nonetheless, their mom and I tried just to stay out of it. I think that the average duration of any one style was less than six months, and by the time it was over, they were usually more tired of it than I was. To me, kids' hair isn't worth a battle. At this writing, both of my kids have hairstyles that I love, and we all love each other and never talk about hair.

Don't meddle needlessly in other people's affairs. Try to avoid fights. Don't throw down the gauntlet unless it's worth the risk. Walk away from what you can. Ask yourself whether or not you will create a long-term enemy by getting into this argument. If it's not all that important to you, forget it, let it go. Let the other person win. Instead, wait for the right moment, the right fight. If you don't fight every battle, people will pay attention when you do mobilize. They will know this must be something really important to you, and you will probably win.

Defuse a situation that is an explosive one. See if you can suck the energy out of it rather than going head to head with a competitor. See if grace and charm can win the day rather than weapons. Join in, befriend them, and wait for your moment to influence them from the inside.

When I talk about going with the flow, it doesn't mean you have to be a coward, only that you don't have to be a bully. It's easier to work with other people than to fight them. Take the time and energy you would normally put into a fight and use it instead to focus the efforts of other people toward the same objective. You all will get there much easier and much faster. Understand there are times you will need to retreat—but never give up on the real wars that define your life.

We need to see when we have a problem to solve rather than a decision to make. We know that we must proceed purposefully and take conscious action in very deliberate ways. We know that doing so will yield results that we will smile about. We know, too, that thinking and action, deciding, solving, researching, or suspending judgment are very different skills that should be used at very different times. And finally, we know that we can learn to use each of these skills in the appropriate moment if we will just pause for a split second and ask, "How am I going to go about deciding this?" or "What process can I use to solve this?" then we know to listen quietly for the answer and discipline ourselves to follow it to a happy outcome.

Select doable tasks. Start with the easy ones. Take action—and in the process, make successes out of other people. Pick your fights carefully. The really successful people are the ones who never pick up the weapons at all. They simply dare to act in ways that change the world.

Think of a time in your life when you were confronted with a "Rubicon," a moment when you, like Julius Caesar, were called upon to act decisively. Did you follow chapter seven's key business practices?

- *Did you pause to determine which skill you needed as you confronted the challenge?*

- *Did you gather the facts you needed? Did you move on in a timely fashion from the fact-gathering process—or did you gather more and more facts to postpone moving ahead?*

- *Did you define your problem?*

- *Did you act your way to a solution—rather than waiting for the solution before you acted?*

- *Did you pick the time and place for your battles with care?*

Which of these gave you the most difficulty? If you failed to put any of these into practice, how can you remind yourself to do better in the future?

Eight

You may not have luck, but you must have pluck

Seek out opportunity and fully exploit it;
ready your roles for what may come next.

You may not be basking in the security of wealth or intellectual brilliance. So what? You can look inside yourself to discover success and start developing it through practice, discipline, and self-development. Success depends less on the big breakthroughs than on *pluck*—an evergreen commitment to personal growth and long-term skill development.

USING YOUR SKILLS

Successful businesses use persistence, patience, and follow-up to reach their goals. When you, too, use these three skills, you will find yourself achieving far more than you ever dreamed.

The story goes that the famous Israeli violinist, Itzhak Perlman, had just completed a brilliant concert when an admirer rushed up to exclaim, "I would give my life to play like that."

"I have," was Perlman's reply.

People hear Perlman's rich tonality and technical mastery, his expressive use of the bow, and amazing repertoire and think his talent is simply a divine gift. But they're wrong. Yes, God did give a wonderful musical talent to Perlman, but Perlman's greatest gift is the tenacity he used to develop that raw talent every day of his life. However brilliant his talent was at age four, it wasn't the stuff of Carnegie Hall. That came with years of development—years and years.

Persistence. What a wonderful thing on which to build a life. Whatever your talent, find a way to work it and develop it every day as part of your routine. This is why the sages of the ages have told us not to give up. They don't mean we should persist once the marketplace has turned a resounding thumbs-down to our new product introduction. They mean when one endeavor fails, you persist in developing the technology behind another new product. Wisdom doesn't say not to give up any particular idea. It says not to give up on yourself!

Never surrender in your efforts to grow and try and strive. Keep getting up every morning to make the world and yourself a little better. With persistence, you can pick up after a fall and rebound with grace. With persistence, you can access creativity that would otherwise be unavailable to you. With persistence, you might be able to reach down and pull from yourself one more try that nobody knew was there. And that try might be "the one," that final, last-ditch effort that sends you over the top.

The philosopher Voltaire said, "No problem can stand the assault of sustained thinking." And this is true. Notice he didn't say that no problem could sustain the assault of brilliance. And the reason is clear. Most of life's opportunities are gained not by a flash of insight (although that is helpful), but by systematic and repeated attempts to chip away at a thing until it is solved.

This is how businesses solve problems and take advantage of opportunities. Success is not about the brilliant insight or the big idea. It is about a big vision and years of work to accomplish it. Companies understand they must find a way to find their way. They do not believe that the competitor down the street is more gifted, more talented, or ordained from above to special success status. They know the future is in their own hands, and they must take responsibility for their actions and their failures to act. They know they must make a plan and then work it.

Of course there are people who are smarter than you. But the exceptional ones have read and studied and read and studied for what would seem like a lifetime to most of us. It is a persistent myth that excellent performance comes by chance.

Look at a person considered to be one of the most talented human beings ever to walk the earth: Wolfgang Amadeus Mozart. Yes, he was a child prodigy. He spoke foreign languages and entertained the emperor when he was only five. But he needed years at the keyboard to be able to create the music for which he is remembered. As a child, he was a curiosity to the court. As a young man who had spent his entire youth working on his technique and style, he was even more amazing.

Forget the idea that someone else out there is more talented or gifted. Start what you plan to do and keep working on it every day. This is what the successful corporations do. Their competitive advantages are rooted in daily efforts to improve their processes and practices. As in sports and in business, life is a game of inches. The winner is just a hair faster, smarter, more interesting, or more colorful.

The best companies in the world also understand that repetition is what persuades the buyer to trade her resources for the payoffs imbued in their product. Every child understands how to launch the repetitive assault no parent can withstand. But somehow we lose that ability to place our repetitions exactly where we need them. Get the skill back. Kids do it. Firms do it. You can do it.

Good salespeople know they may need years to crack open an account. Tenacity wins the day. But smart salespeople in good companies don't just beat their heads against the wall. They listen to the objections of the customer and make adjustments in their presentations here and there to hit a chord with the prospect. If the intended consumer is not interested in the product or service offered, a company will continue to reposition it or repackage it until it is more in tune with what the market seeks. They don't give up, but they don't just try the same old thing over and over, either. That's craziness, not persistence.

You've heard companies talk about their commitment to continuous improvement. This is what you must do. Emulate the companies. Who cares if someone is taller, smarter, or faster? You can win the race the way the proverbial turtle beat the hare. And one day, people will look at you and say, "She is so lucky to be so successful," or "I wish I had his good fortune." And you can chuckle, knowing you took twenty years to become what they think is an overnight sensation.

Success is not an inheritance. The road is a long and arduous one. You're not going to wake up one morning and find yourself a success. Instead, you must wake up each morning and get cracking, so at night when you fall into bed you will close your eyes peacefully, knowing that you inched your way toward your success that day.

Persistence and patience may seem like irreconcilable talents, but they're not. You need to keep your objectives in mind and continually move toward them—and that sometimes means you should do nothing. Sometimes you need to watch and wait. You want to be aggressive when the situation calls for that approach, but patient and ready all the time. This is the stealthy behavior employed by the big cats of Africa. The cheetah doesn't run around the savanna all day. It waits for its moment to strike.

Part of the trick to staying with a task long term is the quiet knowledge of when to back off and let things develop. The changes in the market are what give companies their opportunities. Patience is as big a part of persistence as is decisive action. Sometimes, you simply have to wait until the competition shows a weakness or a new development emerges. And then move in and run like a cheetah.

Follow-up, a cousin of both patience and persistence, is a semiprecious stone that is frequently overlooked because it seems boring. But this mundane little skill is

WHAT WE HAVE DONE HAS BARELY SCRATCHED THE SURFACE. IT TURNS OUT THAT THERE IS, IN FACT, UNLIMITED JUICE IN THAT LEMON. THE FACT IS, THIS IS NOT ABOUT SQUEEZING ANYTHING AT ALL: IT IS ABOUT TAPPING AN OCEAN OF CREATIVITY, PASSION AND ENERGY THAT, AS FAR AS WE CAN SEE, HAS NO BOTTOM AND NO SHORES.

—JACK WELCH

important to the wheels of commerce! And it is important to you. You'll never know what you'll miss if you fail to follow up and find out what is going on right now. The world may have gotten ready for you overnight. Go find out.

Persistence, patience, and follow-up are concepts that help explain why colleges look favorably on candidates who have earned the Eagle Scout Badge. Fewer than 2 percent of all Scouts receive this distinction, but in addition to the accomplishment it signifies, it denotes unusual consistency in an adolescent. It represents long-standing commitment to a goal. It requires effort every week from the time a boy enters a scout troop.

Eagle Scouts are respected not so much because any single requirement is tremendously difficult, nor because the skills needed are exceptional or rare. Only 2 percent of the kids earn it because only 2 percent of the kids are able to form a goal for themselves when they are young and stick with it long enough to emerge with the brass ring. It is about follow-up—as well as persistence and patience. Together, these make a pattern for successful living.

If you want to succeed, start developing the skills you will need to generate payoffs in life. Do it every day. And don't give up.

❧

USING FAILURE TO YOUR ADVANTAGE

Successful companies are resilient. If you accept and utilize life's ups and downs, you too can use "failure" to your advantage.

If you look through the pages of *Business Week* or the *Wall Street Journal,* you will find that the stories behind most successful enterprises include an element of persistence, patience, and follow-up. The converse is also true: Most business failures have to do with some inability or refusal to wait things out patiently or persistently and to follow up on important details. Failing companies get desperate and leap to action—any action—and they fail faster.

We always try to get to the end of a thing. But the world isn't about "The End," like the movies would have you believe. We are on a wild ride in life, and it always keeps moving and metamorphosing. Sometimes it's a roller coaster that takes us up and down. Sometimes it flows into a merry-go-round that cycles round and round. Sometimes it's the tilt-a-whirl that does a little bit of both. In reality, life is not about those endings from the fairy tales in which everyone lived happily ever after. It is a process, and we must emulate the corporations that keep the machine primed 24/7. We must go on, no matter what. A downtime is only a failure if we allow it to be.

Life has a rhythm, a pattern; the human experience really does undulate, just like we see the cycles of business. Sometimes you are on the high side and sometimes you're on the way down. A children's song reminds me of this:

> *The Grand old Duke of York,*
> *He had ten thousand men.*
> *He marched them up the hill*
> *And then he marched them down again.*
> *And when you're up, you're up.*
> *And when you're down, you're down.*
> *And when you're only halfway up,*
> *You're neither up nor down.*

It helps me sometimes to sing this little ditty I learned in first grade, because when you're at the bottom, you know you will have to climb up, and when you are riding the curve on the high side, you will eventually peak and move back down. You have to recognize exactly where you are on the curve, so you won't kid yourself.

Positive thinking and a good attitude are great qualities, but when you're down, you're down. And the first thing to do when you're down there is to recognize where you are. Only then can you do something about it. Denial accomplishes nothing. Positive managers at innovative, open-minded companies recover much more quickly from commercial trauma than do negative, stymied managements. Happy people are more resilient in their personal affairs than are the melancholy. You may lose a relationship or fail to achieve a short-term goal, but if you know your long-term strategy and persistently follow it, you will win other relationships and goals.

Setbacks of all types are just part of life. Successful people see a world of difference between failure and temporary setbacks. Babe Ruth was not a failure even though he struck out a lot. He kept swinging for the bleachers and grabbed those home runs.

You must persist in the marketplace, not with any particular product or account. You must persist in finding a spouse, not necessarily insist on one with green eyes and blond hair. You must persist in the development of a technology, not in any particular application of it. You must persist in the long hours of practice it takes to play the violin, despite your failure to master a specific song. You must persist in your commitment to lose weight, even if you gain a couple of pounds over the holidays. You must persist in your faith, whether or not you stumble or struggle with a certain issue.

What you must do is achieve the goal. The strategies and tactics may rise and fall, but never surrender the objective. And, as they say, don't sweat the small stuff. Most of it *is* small stuff. Separate the insignificant details from the central core of what your life is about; protect and encourage that core, persisting in its development at all costs. Do at least one thing very well. This is the essence of a good life.

Now some people think that those who refuse to accept defeat are fools. And there are many who foolishly persist. Henry Ford, for instance, a brilliant innovator in many ways, was completely wrong to persist in making only black cars well into the 1920s, when people clearly were asking for color choices. Instead of being in the business of moving people around in their choice of vehicles, he got himself hooked on the black car business—and he wouldn't let go. Later, the same company persisted in developing the Edsel, even in the face of significant data to indicate it was a vehicle the consumers no longer wanted. Business has plenty of examples of persistence misapplied. Ford's company eventually got back on track and went back to searching for the right ways for people to move themselves around.

Persist in the goal, not in the specific application. The color could be wrong, the wheel track could be wrong, or the style could be wrong. But that doesn't mean that Ford shouldn't be in the auto business. Kids selling lemonade on the street corner may have a bad experience, but they shouldn't decide this means they aren't cut out for commerce or cooking. They are not failures. They just need a better idea in order to scratch their entrepreneurial itch. Maybe they need to add cookies or Popsicles to their offerings. Maybe their signage or location, pricing or presentation were poor. They should persist until they find the right formula for success.

When we face what looks like failure, we sometimes persist in a silly tactic that has outlived its usefulness. My advice is always try, always continue, but find a new way to attack the problem. Don't just run harder at the immovable object. Climb over it. Dig under it. Give it a wide berth and go around it. Don't beat your head against the wall and call it persistence. That's only giving persistence a bad name and you a headache. That is not perseverance; it's stubbornness. Try, but try something different. Better yet, keep trying, and keep trying different things. Keep the goal, but change the tactic.

Fortunately, companies continued to work on the technology to can foods, make zippers, and grow cultured pearls long after their first attempts failed. They tried something new and persisted in meeting their goals. The opposite can also happen. I have seen many companies kill a new product idea because it seemed similar to some unsuccessful product they tried in the past. This is a sad misfortune. The two entries are not necessarily related. A business should no sooner abandon a marketplace because its previous product bombed than a boy should give up girls because his last date was a flop. Better companies do not abandon a strategy just because of poor execution the last time out of the box. They fix what was wrong with their execution! This requires that a company be frank and honest about its mistakes, write off the losses, and go on to bigger and better things.

Use your energy and creative juices to think of new ways to get past that stubborn object. When a company's people are too bound up in a problem to crack it, the company will often call in a consultant to help it think about the problem from a new direction. And you shouldn't hesitate to ask for outside help from a friend, a religious leader, a therapist, or any wise old sage who's handy. There is no shame in not having all the answers.

The only wrong answer is to do the same thing over and over again and expect a better or different result. Instead, find a new approach. Be resilient—*and* creative.

~⚮~

EVALUATING THE RISK

Successful businesses accept that some risks are necessary stepping-stones to success. In a similar way, individuals should evaluate and accept life's necessary risks.

Just as you shouldn't be afraid to make mistakes, you shouldn't be afraid to take risks.

You shouldn't fear only necessary risks, of course. A common misconception about risk is that entrepreneurs are the personification of risk-taking. That is bunk. Entrepreneurs who have survived to sport gray hair only do so because they have carefully organized their universe to corral their risks. They don't pretend that the risks don't exist; they just organize their companies to avoid the pitfalls.

> THE ONLY PEOPLE
> WHO NEVER FAIL
> ARE THOSE WHO
> NEVER TRY.
> —ILKA CHASE

Individuals, however, tend to avoid all risks in the vain hope for security. Forget it. The greatest security you can ever enjoy will come the day you decide to take control of your life, build a plan, take some action, test the results of that plan, and inch your way into taking the prudent risks that will make you free to enjoy life.

Life is never risk free. If you pick the right goals, wholesome objectives, and good strategies, you will still hit many bumps in the road. Keep your eyes on the prize and continue to strive toward the ultimate good as you see it. Don't be sidetracked by the many bad things that could befall you, and don't give up on a good plan just because bad weather is predicted. Despite the risks, keep studying, continue practicing, and persist in developing yourself.

You'll never experience success in your life roles if you're unwilling to accept the risks that go along with them. Keep an eye out, remain calm, follow up your leads, and keep trying. Success will give itself to you if you are open to receiving it on its terms, not yours.

Make a Plan that Makes Sense

The sounder the business strategy is and the more sense it makes, the greater the number of mistakes that can occur without harming the enterprise. You, too, can afford more mistakes if your overall plan makes sense.

If you have an excellent strategy, your execution can, in fact, be a little less effective and still achieve acceptable results. The opposite is, of course, that if you have an essentially flawed strategy, all of the confidence in the world can't pull it off; even the most brilliant management won't make headway. If a business proposition is essentially weak, if it doesn't make sense to the marketplace, it will fail to achieve profitability. Furthermore, it will waste resources that could be used for much better ventures.

Figure out what needs to be done, figure out a way to get it done, and then work on doing it efficiently. So many times, people and companies go straight to the fine-tuning when it isn't clear that the marketplace has even a remote interest in what they're trying to develop. One of the easiest ways to win an argument, however, is to be right in the first place. And if you're right, you can stumble over your words, mess up your hair, or even annoy some people. But if your message is essentially flawed, the most perfect delivery will not allow you to win the day.

Now don't get me wrong; you still have to pull things off well. The difference between the winners and the also-rans is not necessarily only confidence. You still must spell the words right on your packaging, get the color of your logo right, and present your message in a way the world can understand. All of those basic skills and competencies are important in the business world and in our personal lives. But the strategy has to be basically correct. It has to be something the world wants, or all the perfect, glitzy, and sophisticated techniques won't be able to bring success.

Get out there with what is right, right now. You will have plenty of time to make adjustments. Some of the very best gardeners I know focus on making sure the plants they have are healthy. So what if there are some weeds in the yard, who cares? If it's worth doing in the first place, it might be that it's worthwhile even if it is not perfect. The other side of that would be: If it isn't worth doing in the first place, doing it perfectly achieves nothing. People and companies need to make sure the sweeping strategy is right before they fine-tune a result. You can't fix with efficiency what is ineffective. You can always fix with effectiveness what is inefficient.

Typically, the focus is on how we can do things better. The real questions are: Do we need to do it at all? Should we be doing something else instead? In your life and in your business you probably already know what is counterproductive. Determine the things that are not in the interests of your corporate or personal strategies and begin to eradicate them. Being organized gives you time to think about the long-term strategic issues for yourself or your company. And some strategies require efficiency.

One way to be efficient in personal relationships is to develop credibility over time. That credibility enables you to go straight to the heart of the matter with the people who know you. That creates astounding efficiency. The credibility you enjoy, however, comes from doing the right things for people over time, not necessarily by dealing with them the most efficiently. Be clear on which things are your strategies' goals—and which are simply by-products of those strategies.

You want to develop and operate under conditions that are favorable. If you want a large reward in the form of monetary compensation, the best strategy is not to focus on money, but instead focus on what people want. The old saw says the way to really enjoy a meal is to come to the table hungry. If you apply that logic to your life you'll see the sense. Even the most perfectly prepared meal in the world won't have much appeal to people who have no appetite. You have to find what the world is hungry for. Companies do that; it's called market research. You can do it, too, in each of your roles. For instance, would your children prefer a spotless environment or more quality time with you? Would your parents like a lot of expensive gifts from you or would they be more pleased if you took time for regular phone calls? Find out what the people in your life really want.

A fantasy runs through the American work ethic that if you confidently go about the business of working hard, paying a lot of attention to specifics, excellent payoffs will happen automatically.

The most important thing to ask in the very beginning is whether all this work is dedicated toward achieving worthwhile ends. Often it is not; that's the problem with fantasy.

Another good strategy is not to plan every detail. Instead, shape the odds in your favor. Find out what isn't working well and figure out how to amend the situation. See where the competition is weak or what opportunities are most immediate. Decide how you can quickly offer something to serve a need. Doing it well can come later.

This is the thinking to use when you buy a house. The rule is buy the neighborhood, not the house; in the long run the house is the most changeable variable in the equation. Ultimately, you can totally reconstruct your home, but not the neighborhood. The best strategic thinker buys the least improved and cheapest home in a nice neighborhood. That way you have no way to go but up. Don't focus on the perfect house; focus on finding the neighborhood that is right.

Similarly, if you're not achieving the kind of results you'd like in your career, the first thing to look at isn't your specific failings. Instead, determine whether the things you're good at have been properly applied. You may be in the wrong kind of work. You may be working for the wrong kind of company. Maybe you have a personality conflict either with the management of the company or with the industry in which you are working. Don't start worrying that you can't perform well at *any* job. You may merely be a square peg who is round-holing it.

This also is true when you're looking to get a book published or find a loan. Don't assume that just because one publisher or one banker says no to your proposition that others will do the same. If you really have done your homework and feel like the marketplace will embrace your strategy, you need to get the message out. The right place for you and your plan is in the office of the person who already ascribes to this kind of thinking. Find this person because they already believe in your mission. The rest will flow like pure poetry.

In your career, the best strategy is to find the kind of work to which you are best adapted because of your nature, interests, and personality. That is 90 percent of success. Work hard, persistently and intelligently, on the other 10 percent. Together, talent and effort will deliver success, whether for a company or an individual.

<hr/>

KNOWING THE TRENDS

Successful businesses go with the flow. You, too, should know today's trends—and use them.

There are all kinds of personal applications to this kind of thinking. Going with the flow at the personal level means you carefully choose your environment and the kind of people with whom you spend time, because over the years you're going to become more and more like your associates and friends. Putting yourself in contact with people you want to emulate is one way to manage your personal growth. You're likely to adapt to their styles and amend your behavior in ways that will please you. Put yourself in the right strategic place to take advantage of a positive life stream. You also have to put yourself in an atmosphere where you can achieve. Don't knock your head against the wall. It is far more important to understand your limits and what you do well than to try to "discipline" yourself to change.

Remember, the world is always changing. Constantly ask yourself if this endeavor is still worthwhile. Is this role something others still want from me? You have to be especially careful if you have had success in a certain area. Don't make it a sacred cow that keeps you from finding the right direction. Don't be a motorboat that revs upstream no matter what; be sensitive to the currents around you.

Just like playing a musical instrument: most people quit before the melodies begin to flow. When most people leave the field, that is your opportunity. Give yourself a chance by practicing the drills, encouraging your capabilities, and enduring in making the pursuit of your ultimate goals part of your daily life. Work to find the environment in which you can achieve. Fate may not have smiled on you with some uniquely leverageable ability, highly marketable talent, or rich relatives, but determination and "pluck" compensates for these deficiencies. People who diligently persist will find the deck stacked in their favor, rewarding their dogged determination and meticulous preparation.

Write down a goal in your life you have yet to achieve. Now examine that goal in light of chapter eight's key business practices:

- *Have you used persistence, patience, and follow-up to attain this goal?*

- *How can you use past or current "failures" to help you achieve the goal?*

- *What risks are entailed with achieving this goal? Are those risks acceptable? In the past, have you allowed the risks to hold you back?*

- *Do you have a sound strategy in place for achieving your goal? If not, what do you need to do to formulate one?*

- *How can you use life's already existing currents to propel you toward your goal?*

Nine

IF YOU'RE BARKING UP THE WRONG TREE, MORE YELP WON'T HELP

Improve performance via feedback;
make it painless for others to tell you the truth.

If you're barking up the wrong tree, you're just wasting your voice. Don't be the old dog stuck with outdated tricks. Life should be a process of constant learning and growth. Sniff out information about what you're doing right and what you need to work on. Lift those floppy ears and listen to the people around you. Don't be afraid of criticism; if you got a pat on the head for everything you did, you'd never improve or excel. Encourage people to be honest with you. A meaty nugget of honest feedback is more valuable than a bowl of sweet compliments. If all signs are telling you there's nothing interesting in that tree you're barking at, give it up. *More yelp won't help.*

LISTENING TO FEEDBACK

Successful businesses welcome complaints. In your life, recognize that new interpersonal dilemmas are also just fresh answers trying to express themselves.

Pay attention to the complaints from people who rely on you, the criticism from your peers, and the verbal attacks of your adversaries. These are goldmines. Through them, people are telling you how to improve yourself and bind yourself more closely to your objectives. Take them up on their challenges. Get proactive about bringing in complaints. Make sure that the people who offer them feel heard and understood, and let them know what you're going to do about the problem.

Some companies have set up toll-free numbers to collect complaints from their customers. As

> DIFFICULTIES ARE
> MEANT TO ROUSE,
> NOT DISCOURAGE.
> —WILLIAM ELLERY
> CHANNING

an individual you should emulate these companies' example. Make it easy for people to complain about you. Don't get angry, don't get irritated, and don't rush to defend yourself. Just listen. Make it easy for people to tell you what's wrong so you can fix it.

Unsolicited or unwarranted complaints may be hard to take, but they're valuable—the unsolicited because it's a gift, the unwarranted because regardless of whether it's true, somebody perceives it to be true. The fact that someone cares enough to pass the message along proves you're important to them. The situation may turn into a positive event that will cement your relationship for a long time.

Get out there and ask people what you're doing wrong and how you can improve—and then do it. Give people positive feedback about what they've said to you. Give them progress reports and make sure they understand it was their comments that caused you to make these improvements. Make them feel deputized now and forevermore to let you know if you're getting off track. These people will love to help you out.

As I've said earlier, most of your customers—probably five out of six—won't grouse; they'll just leave. The same may be true in your personal life. Listen carefully for clues that others are unhappy with you. Silence may mean others are quietly giving up on you.

A complaint is a potent signal from a concerned loyalist. Disregard the style. Listen to the message. We all have a tendency, at work or in our personal lives, to imagine that a complaint is being generated by hostile weirdos. It's probably just the opposite. Very few people care enough to complain. To complain means they've thrown their lot in with you enough to spend energy on trying to improve you.

It's hard to accept a complaint that doesn't fit in with our view of our company or ourselves. Try to listen well enough to under-stand what is actually being said. Don't feel a need to respond immediately. Assume the comments are being made by people who have your best interest at heart. Write down what was said and put it away for a few days so you can come up with some responses.

Another thing you could do is share the complaint with someone less emotionally involved in the situation. It could be a coworker, an objective friend, or some other person whose judgment you respect, such as a clergyperson or mentor. Ask that person to help you deci-pher the elements of truth in the complaint.

When you get a complaint, find out what the person wants and what she wants you to do about it. Know what she expects before and after the complaint. Repeat the complaint back to her; it helps you understand the situation and reassures her that you're listening.

Give her immediate recognition that you have processed what she has said, but also give her regular status reports on what is taking place until the situation is corrected.

When customers, employees, friends, or even my spouse have complaints, I've found it very effective to ask (in the most nonthreatening way I can manage at the moment) what the problem is and what they would they like me to do about it now and in the future. And if they have the patience for all this, I ask what they think I could have done to prevent the problem in the first place. If the passion of the moment keeps you from thinking clearly, don't be embarrassed to go back later and get these questions answered. That information will be both the road map to solving the problem and a way for you to measure your progress.

But, as always, be honest. Do not build false expectations. Don't promise to fix something if you really can't or won't do it. This is a corollary to the old advertising adage that it makes no sense to advertise or manufacture any product that cannot deliver the promise in the marketplace.

Committing to a life of continuous improvement, based on experimentation and feedback is far more a path to success than lucking into any one action or decision. It boggles my mind when I speak with successful people who try to explain their success in terms of some decision they made. I'm astounded that people look

> AT EVERY STAGE OF OUR LIVES, WHATEVER IS CROWDING OUT GROWTH NEEDS TO BE RECOGNIZED AND REMOVED.
> —JEAN SHINODA BOLEN

back and say, "Our company grew because we made this decision" or "We were profitable because we made that deal" or "I grew as a person because I did this or that." In my experience, the reality is that people and companies succeed not because of any single event or even a series of spectacular events. Instead, success is due to a certain attitude, a certain frame of mind, one that includes listening to feedback. Success comes when we try to understand, relate to, and therefore better serve the people around us.

At some point years ago, the successful people of today must have intently listened, and then they reacted quickly and gave others what was necessary at the time. Whether they painted the wall blue, married George, or introduced the most spectacular new product the industry had ever seen, what happened was the result of a sensitivity they had developed. They had set their antennae to understand and process the events around them, and they translated that into appropriate actions at the moment. It was the process they pursued that caused the decision to which they now credit their success.

Companies and people need to learn this. It's not actions, but the way in which you relate, that brings success. Every decision, every activity, and every pursuit has a life cycle. That which is to last must be built on a tradition of responsiveness, of developing and delivering what is worthwhile.

❧

IGNORING ADVICE

Successful businesses have learned to filter their feedback. There are some kinds of advice you, too, should ignore.

You need to examine and understand each complaint. That's the only way to ensure you've been open-minded and aren't letting personal feelings of anger or irritation get in the way. But this is not to say you have to act on every complaint. You don't want to be swayed by every harsh wind—and

REMEMBER THAT 20 PERCENT OF THE PEOPLE ARE AGAINST EVERYTHING ALL THE TIME.
—ROBERT KENNEDY

to avoid that, you need to filter out some kinds of complaints.

The first kind of complaint you should usually disregard is the negative nay-saying of the crusty old curmudgeon. The world is full of gruff old fossils who are about to break their arms patting themselves on the back because they have "experience." When someone tells you to step back and get in line behind them because they have experience, find out first whether their encounters with life have any relevance to what you are contemplating. See if their careers were positive or negative. Usually, you'll find these people are vortexes of negative energy centered on something they tried years ago and failed. Don't listen to this type of experience. It will only discourage you. It has nothing to do with what's happening now. It's a trap that will lead you to do nothing. You have to make a future for yourself. You don't do that by listening to the sour warnings of people who never got off the ground themselves. It is a trap to listen to old sourpusses who want to tell you exactly what not to do.

The second trap to avoid is listening to successful people who want to tell you exactly what to do. Remember that the actions that brought them success in 1974 are unlikely to get more than modest results today. With the world changing so quickly (and you being so very different from anyone else), it's really not smart to begin or abandon work on your dream just because someone else succeeded or failed under very different circumstances.

Obviously, we all have a lot to learn, and you can do it by picking up pointers from those who have gone before us. Just choose wisely. The best method I have for deciding whom to respect is to imagine that person at my age and in my circumstances. If he seems like the kind of person I was or am trying to be, then I'm inclined to listen to his advice. If I cannot relate to him as a person of my age, and if he certainly isn't who I want to be at his age, I don't take much stock in his advice. Why? Because his advice, if followed, will cause me to be more like him and less like me. And that's not what I want. I can ask this kind of guy for directions to the ballpark or his recipe for barbecued ribs, but I don't ask him about marriage or family matters.

Be open to feedback—but pass it carefully through the sieve of common sense.

~⁊~

EXPERIMENTING WITH IDEAS

Successful businesses experiment with new products through market testing. Use a similar technique in your personal life as a valuable tool for working with new ideas.

Market testing helps us find out whether a prototype will work the way we expect. It's a way to play around with a concept before we invest a ton of money in inventory and ship it all over the world. It's a low-cost, low-risk tool for learning more about a product before we take a leap.

As you contemplate your life, what can you do to explore your options before fully committing? This process is actually quite routine. You go on dates (hopefully plenty) before you commit to marriage. You visit a college before you commit to four years there. You certainly test-drive a new car before you buy.

However, when it comes to a pet idea, either as a business or an individual, we tend to rush into giving 100 percent. This is lunacy. The immediate choice is not between taking on a project or rejecting it. There is a gray area, a middle ground we should explore. We need to try the concept on for size, looking at the potential consequences before we fully commit to a new idea.

At some point in the late sixties, American car manufacturers came around to accepting the ideas advocated by emerging consumer groups. Enter the crash-test dummies. Everyone at the time wondered why the real dummies hadn't thought of a crash test up until then. Scientific testing and organized experimentation with model cars is now standard operating procedure. The idea is to understand and address safety concerns before the model goes into production.

> NO PLAN EMERGES UNSCATHED FROM ITS COLLISION WITH REALITY.
> —SHIRLEY ABBOTT

There is no shame in failing one of your own in-house tests. It's good business to find out about the problem early, while there is still time to change the plan. Just be sure to budget in enough time to fix the problems you discover. Test with zest. Isn't it better to find out about a problem while the product is still being tested than it would be to jump in and have your dumb design pointed out later in *Consumer Reports*?

Test results must be duplicated; one time down the path is not enough. If you can't replicate your positive test results, consider them a benign aberration. If you and Mark have gone out seven times, but he was only fun on the first date, then forget him. Results have to be reproduced to be valuable.

Years ago, architectural sophisticates began using computer technology to help clients grasp the three-dimensional space being designed for them. The future occupants were shown a computer simulation of their new space. If they hated the walls because they were red, not blue, it could be changed with the push of a button. Now you can walk into any software retailer and buy consumer versions of these industrial-strength architectural tools. You can see how your new landscaping, roofline, or doghouse will look before you actually implement the project.

In your personal life, go out of the way to test your ideas as well. Send up trial balloons. Try out a thing out before you bet the farm. Don't let yourself get so caught up in the passion of forging ahead, that you forget this aspect of the process.

Testing isn't that tough. You need a little bit of systematic thinking, some rudimentary scientific process, and a good deal of honesty to be able to look frankly at the results and decide whether you're staring at a fluke or the real McCoy. Take the time to do it. You'll save time in the long run, and you can retrench or retreat without losing either face or your wallet.

A model or prototype is always a good idea. Sometimes consumers just don't realize what is possible, so they'll give very bland answers when asked what kind of product they would like. But if you put a new Apple iMac in front of them, they can tell you whether they like the size of the keyboard, whether the machine should be teal or lime, and whether the Internet connection is as easy as it was made out to be. By the same token, if you're considering accepting a new job with a demanding and complicated schedule, you might want to try driving there some morning at rush hour so you can experience the schedule's real-life effects on your home life.

Testing your ideas on real people is not for the faint of heart. People can be brutal with their feedback on your pet idea, whether it's for a new family menu, a color-coordinated organizational system

> WE HAD TO PICK OURSELVES UP AND GET ON WITH IT, DO IT ALL OVER AGAIN, ONLY EVEN BETTER THIS TIME.
>
> —SAM WALTON

for your home, or a professional change in direction. You must actively seek comments from the people who will be central to a plan's implementation. The key is to be intellectually honest enough to hear the feedback without getting defensive.

Don't spend a nickel on a test that you can't afford to lose. If you can't afford the test, how can you afford the full-blown rollout? If, however, you can afford the test, and if it proves successful, you'll have results you can use to persuade other people to bankroll you! Buy them into your process and they will have a vested interest in your success.

Make room for plenty of leeway. Don't box yourself in during any test. It is precisely a test because you are still trying to figure out how best to do it. Why chisel it in stone? And since you are doing live research, you must be careful about your conclusions. Don't tear down the restaurant because the meals are lousy. Get a new cook. Don't give up altogether when the problem may be one small and fixable variable. You are testing certain variables. If you find the results unsatisfactory, be careful to fix only what is specifically wrong. Keep trying, but keep trying something other than the things that have already come up short.

❦

Valuing Feedback

An impediment to business success is a mindset characterized by the phrase "steady as she goes." As an individual, you need to be flexible enough to respond to life's feedback.

Despite the many arguments for flexibility over rigid thick-headedness, we still have people who believe changing their mind is a character flaw. They think it's a mistake to *ever* bend to the changing wind.

This kind of thinking means we somehow think that changing our course to take advantage of a new current would make us a failure. We don't want to change our college major in English, even though emerging opportunities in the human genome project excite us more. We see it as disloyal to change employers, even though the job we agreed to is no longer the reality. We feel like failures if we abandon a project, even though the payoff no longer supports it. We cling to outdated goals as though they were a matter of honor. Steady as she goes . . . right into the iceberg!

One reason for this trap is that we may have invested our time, our resources, our reputations, our "worth" into a particular course of action—and we feel we have to squeeze out something of value or we will have toiled in vain. The better corporations understand this and have an axiom to fight it: "Sunk costs are sunk." What you have already put in is already put in. The blood, sweat, and tears have been spilled. Now what is the best thing to do? Is it best to go on or to do something else?

Think in terms of fixing an old car. Something breaks, you take it in, and they fix it at a cost of $500. You drive it for two weeks only to have another part go out. The cost to repair it will be another $500. You're teetering on the edge of buying a new car when you remember that you spent $500 just two weeks ago. You hate to "throw away" the money you've already invested.

Here's where it gets tricky. Forget the previous $500. Look only at the choices available to you now and what future each choice will bring you. If spending $500 more will fix the problem, then spend the money. If you think you have a lemon, you should choose a new car. In neither case should you look at your past investment to determine what your future investment should be. Sunk costs are sunk.

The very best companies take their markdowns on bad inventory and bad hires as soon as they can. They get the pain behind them and go on to new opportu-

> SOMEONE'S SITTING IN THE SHADE TODAY BECAUSE SOMEONE PLANTED A TREE A LONG TIME AGO.
> —WARREN BUFFET

nities. As we travel down the highways and byways of life, we, too, will certainly take some wrong turns. The biggest mistake we can make, however, is not stopping by the roadside for a minute to figure out where we might be going wrong.

There's a deadly syndrome that can strike fighter pilots. It's called "target fixation," a trancelike state in which the pilot zones in on the crosshairs so intently that he fails to pull up from the target in time to recover his altitude. He ends up crashing into the very object he was sent to take out. Sometimes we, too, become so focused on the goal that we no longer know where we are.

Never fail because you've become fixated, blindly trying the same thing over and over, expecting different results. If you can't say you would have started dating Mary if you knew then what you know now, or would have taken job B if you knew then what you know now, then you must drop them. If you're getting insufficient return on your investment of heartache or work, pull the plug before you go down the tubes as well.

This is another one of those things that is very simple but not at all easy. Companies, even the greatest, struggle with divestitures. Cutting off the parts of the company that have outlived their usefulness is painful. But it's essential.

There's only so much of you to go around. You can't say a robust "yes" to anything without saying a resounding "no" to the things that aren't working. It is never a mistake to stop doing something that is hurting you. The point is, successful companies—and individuals—know why they are succeeding and why they are losing ground. Losers, on the other hand, are clueless as to why they are slipping. They are out of touch with reality.

And don't assume that particular roles that have worked for you for years will always work for you in exactly the same way. Be sensitive to both internal and external feedback as your roles mature and change. Don't rest on the faulty assumption that a longstanding successful course of action will always be successful. You may find you're putting less in and getting less out. The value of your role has faded—both in your eyes and in the eyes of others.

Of course, you have the choice to milk this role. But think through the future scenarios. Time will inevitably bring still more changes. See how you feel about being in the role in a way that would be radically different from the way you have been operating. Major corporations milk their maturing businesses every day. But they do so with full knowledge of the consequences. They do so "on purpose." You, too, can make that choice—but you, too, should do so only when you have listened to all the feedback you can gather.

If you won't be getting adequate payoffs for what you'll be investing, the decision is obvious. Find other ways to get payoffs from life, using the strengths that are in their ascendancy instead of the ones that are in decline. Seek out new roles. Allow feedback to steer you to more satisfying and productive roles. Change may be painful—but we are never too old for the excitement and rewards of new possibilities. The future is full of potential—but you need to be flexible enough to accept it.

⟋⟋⟍

RESPONDING TO FEEDBACK

Successful businesses understand that listening to feedback is a lifelong process. In our personal lives as well, feedback is a continual process that shapes our success.

Businesses' response to feedback is a time-consuming process, the purpose of which is to envision a successful future for themselves and to work backward from that future to where they are now. They use customer feedback to detail exactly what they have to do today, next year, and five years from now in order to reach their companies' promised land.

Individuals need to do a similar thing. They must then begin to listen to all the relevant feedback. That is the way to amend the wrongs that haunt them, to correct the mistakes they have made and are making, and to take positive steps toward making their dreams a reality.

And remember, the more successful you are, the more problems you're going to have because you'll be entering new situations that haven't shaken down yet. You'll be trail blazing. Accept that and go forward. It's a lot of fun.

Fix the problems that result from your successes. As you grow, excel, or prosper, parts of you may grow callous, indifferent, or tired. You've gotten this far by providing solutions that address needs or fix problems. But your answers won't last forever. Constantly evaluate where yesterday's brainstorm may be today's barrier. The process is never over.

Today is the day to begin using the clues we receive from others to help us close the gap between where we are headed today and where we hope to be at our final hour. That feedback can act as a rudder to steer us into our future. It's a constant process of response and correction as we fine-tune our life course.

So get going. You have miles to go.

Make a list of the five most memorable complaints you have ever received. Human nature being what it is, you'll have the clearest memories of the ones that annoyed you most, that you found most unfounded. Now evaluate each of these complaints in light of chapter nine's key practices for success:

- *What new answers or solutions might you have derived from these complaints?*

- *Should you have filtered out these complaints because of their source? Did you overreact?*

- *How could you have used market testing to find a solution to the problems presented by these complaints?*

- *Did you lack the flexibility needed to respond positively to these complaints? Were you insisting on a "steady as she goes" approach to life?*

- *Is there any way you can respond to these complaints still today? Can you resolve to turn criticism to your advantage, next time?*

Ten

ROLE WITH THE PUNCHES

Sometimes you have to remake yourself or your roles—
and you can do it!

C hange the rules and the whole game becomes different. You'll play differently, you'll plan differently, you'll organize differently. Companies are learning the hard way that who they were does not guarantee who they will be. Smart competitors are no longer following the old rules, and today's marketplace is cheering in the stands. You can go around (and around) in an effort to save time and money, and that's good. Incremental improvement over a long period of time generates rewards. But plodding along, while workable, doesn't mean that you don't look around and grab opportunity when you see it. You leapfrog the rest when you jump on what's best. For your results to improve dramatically, you must first change not only what you are putting into the situation, but you must also change your situation itself! You can work your guts out for a lifetime and just eke out a good living. Or, if you're willing to adapt and change in response to life's "punches," you can leap on top of the heap. Remember from the last chapter: you must be persistent *not* with your activities, but with your dreams. If you find a new and better way to get there, take it! In fact you should *look*.

~≈~

STARTING OVER

Successful companies begin anew when needed. You, too, will create the future you want when you are willing to try a brand-new approach to your age-old goal.

Johann Gutenberg figured it out back in the fifteenth century. When he decided to improve the way Bibles were made, he didn't try to find monks who could pen manuscripts faster or go for ink that would dry more quickly. He didn't try to condense the text into the first *Bible Digest*. Gutenberg wasn't trying to make incremental improvements in the process. He fundamentally changed the way books were reproduced, and in so doing fundamentally changed the world.

Gutenberg came up with using movable metal type to create a reusable and economical system for printing the written word. He borrowed technology from wine pressing and melded it with his system of letter-type—and trumped all other efforts to print books. At that time, no one was even trying to manufacture manuscripts for the masses. Reading was the exclusive province of the aristocracy and the church. Gutenberg's invention created the first mass distribution of the written word and allowed works to be published in the local language, fueling a groundswell of interest in books, especially the Bible. As his texts came into the hands of the common people in their indigenous languages, the stage was set for the Protestant Reformation and the remaking of the history of religious faith.

Gutenberg also made a lot of smaller practical contributions to the process. For example, he gets extra marks because the quality of his work was precise and impeccable. He was also smart to start publishing books in his native tongue . . . but that isn't the reason for his fame. He is remembered for creating a process that leapfrogged the way books had been made for centuries, giving new freedom to printers and publishers to create and distribute content to a world hungry for books. Gutenberg completely changed the rules of publishing and, in so doing, changed the way the world learned, thought, and acted. A pretty important game of leapfrog!

Just think of the huge improvements in printing technology over the past 500 years. The printed page has become more flexible and colorful, produced far more quickly at far less cost. Hundreds of thousands of talented people have made many more thousands of incremental changes to the business. Many have made good livings in these industries, but, other than Gutenberg, few are in the history books. The fame, the fortune, and the payoffs in life come from changing an idea's entire orbit, not mildly improving what already exists.

Worthwhile careers and productive lives can be earned by making things better, bigger, and more responsive. This is good. There will be opportunities in your life to "supersize it," so don't be absent that day. After all, corporations have payrolls to meet and individuals have mortgage payments due.

That means they avoid unnecessary risk. In our personal lives as well, most of us spend a lot of time and energy making sure we stay in our comfort zone, avoiding anything new that might bounce us out of control. But if we let security sit in the driver's seat, we lose control anyway, and wind up just slogging along the path of conformity.

People who fall into that trap are doomed to a life of mediocrity and deny themselves the exhilaration of passion.

Any business that focuses on managing risk, caution, and "downside potential" is really taking the most risky path of all. You can't sustain a business by avoiding risk. You grow and develop as a person by being part of what is going on, not by attempting to avoid it.

Classical MBA-type schooling defines risk and economic realities in models that reinforce this type of "safety" for the corporation's assets. Well, I am here to tell you that a string of only "safe" relationships, whether in your career or personal life, will leave you financially or emotionally bankrupt. Relationships, ideas, or actions that have guaranteed outcomes are usually just piddly things that don't make a difference, anyway.

For fear of the big idea, a person may ignore the personal growth and success that is possible when you commit to something bigger and bolder than yourself. I don't know of any business guru bigger or bolder in the last ten years than Jack Welch, the exceptionally successful former CEO of the General Electric Company. He concluded years ago that companies inexorably slip when they restrict themselves to making incremental improvements while failing to commit to the quantum leap. He exhorted his executives to think big and be bold.

> I AM CONVINCED THAT IF THE RATE OF CHANGE INSIDE AN ORGANIZATION IS LESS THAN THE RATE OF CHANGE OUTSIDE, THE END IS IN SIGHT.
> —JACK WELCH

That is what I say to you, too. The big break may not come

tomorrow or the next day. But it will come if you are vigilant and prepared. Keep your light on. Keep your shoes by your bed; be ready to follow opportunity when it peeks around the corner; and give the intuitive side of you a chance to rule for a while. Find a changing or changeable situation that will give you a competitive advantage; then thrust yourself into it—and don't step back until you've made a positive difference. The best way to improve a life you don't like is to start a new one today.

You may not be able to let go of the familiar and pedestrian life you are leading now. So don't. Just start a relationship with a new life; begin by doing something very different from what you've done before. Your values don't have to change. Most of your beliefs don't have to change. Only your behavior has to change . . . drastically. A big difference between successful and unsuccessful companies is that the ones who succeed are the ones who do what needs to be done, whether they want to or not. Successful companies simply do the things that unsuccessful companies aren't willing to do.

And it's the same with people. Once you detect in yourself the sorrowful mood of opportunity lost, you simply won't be fulfilled by doing more of the same old thing. You must shrug off the tyranny of the familiar and venture out to find the new you, the one who is searching for something bigger and better out of life. If there is a germ of unhappiness in you, the pang of knowing that you could do more, the heartache of not yet reaching your potential, then you must make a decision to live differently. Once you do that, you create a new you. Or you can think of this experience in terms of "personal resurrection"; a part of you that may have seemed dead—a creative, hopeful, powerful part—will spring back to life.

Let me give you a personal example of leapfrog action. In high school I was junior class president, and my job was to put on the sock hops we had after varsity basketball games. A big controversy developed over the type of music we should play. We were still spinning 33⅓ records at this point, along with a few 45s.

Some kids liked one musical group, some liked another. We were always in a mess, and no matter what we did to make everyone happy, nobody was satisfied with the record selection. A competitor who wanted my job announced his plan for choosing the music based on a polling form he hung up in the cafeteria for everyone to see. I was in big trouble. My "play by request" method was not working.

So I sat thinking one night and was struck dumb by the idea that we should roll in a real live band that could play a variety of music. I didn't announce my plan. One night after the big game, my buddies, my girlfriend, and I surprised everyone by bringing out the band, and they started to whoop it up. No one had seen anything like it at our high school.

We added some fun to the night by suspending hundreds of balloons in a huge bag on the ceiling of the gym. I had one clever friend (today you might call him a techno-weenie) who figured out a contraption to release all those colorful balloons just as the music started. This was years before every kid could see balloons drop on TV at every political gathering. The crowd went wild.

Now this little leapfrogging may not sound momentous, but it got me elected student body president, unopposed, while my girlfriend was elected vice president.

As a college student I went back to visit my old school. The guy who was then president of the junior class told me my idea had worked great for a couple of years, but now the kids were fighting over what type of band should be chosen. Some liked soul music, others liked rock 'n' roll.

I told him the model was broken, and he should switch to the idea of using a musical feed from the same local station that broadcast the games. For very little he could get a radio personality to come down and spin the best of what was hot in all types of music, using the station's approved play-list for the first hour and taking requests once the crowd started to thin out. The kid instantly saw the value in leapfrogging out of the current mess. Incrementally changing the situation wasn't going to work! Yep, that guy was elected student council president the next year.

You too can leapfrog your way to success if you remember: persist in your goal . . . change the tactics (a lot).

⸎

CONQUERING FEAR

Successful businesses don't allow fear to keep them from achieving success. Don't let fear rule your life either.

Most people don't do the things they'd really like to do because they lack the fortitude and bravery to do so. Their reasoning is, "If I'm afraid, that means I better not do it." The presence or absence of fear is not a valid indicator of whether you should proceed. Fools do all kinds of dangerous things, and cautious people foolishly fail to do all kinds of safe and reasonable things. Companies are the same way.

But for the vibrant person or business, the really important things are the ones you do in spite of your fear. Things like showing up for your wedding service, finding a new job, or signing your first mortgage. Sure you were scared, but you did it anyway. These acts took courage; they asked you to leave your familiar comfort zone and venture out into the unknown. Go with your knees rattling if you have to . . . but go!

Companies get into new and unfamiliar businesses every day. They must do so to have the future they envision (or any future at all). You also must get into new, uncomfortable situations and relationships on a regular basis if you want to live the type of life you have chosen for yourself.

<hr/>

Choosing Your Future

Successful companies make decisions in the context of what they want to become. You, too, should make choices based on the future you want to have.

Adapting yourself to life's punches doesn't mean you relinquish control of your life to circumstances. Just the opposite, in fact. It comes down to a quiet reflection on the question "Who is in charge of my life?" There are four choices:

1. You can rely on people or influences totally outside of yourself.

2. You can rely on the person you have been up until now.

3. You can rely on the person you are right now.

4. You can choose the fourth and best option: Let the person you hope to become make the decisions about what you should do and when you should do it.

Decide to listen more closely to that future self. This means exerting self-discipline and a willingness to act on what you know is good for yourself. Most companies are far better at this than individuals. They allocate resources to the emerging market opportunities. Follow that path.

The really terrific thing about being a human is that the moment you take a step to improve yourself, progress begins immediately, and improvement will follow improvement as long as you continue the effort. We humans change by doing. This truth will set you free. We are driven largely by habit, and the only way to end a habit is to substitute a new habit that fits in with the future you want for yourself.

If you want to change a little, make some little changes. You'll feel great. If you want (or need) to change a lot, put yourself on a plan to remake yourself, and it will happen as long as you continue to act in the new way instead of the old. If you want to control your future, control the way you act at this very moment and for the rest of the day. Do that every day for the rest of your life, and you can be whatever you dream. You must actively walk into the life you select by starting to be a new person today.

Companies have learned that bad situations usually don't get better by themselves. When things sour, most corporations act right away and don't dillydally, hoping the situation will improve. The same is true for companies that realize, however slowly or painfully, that their current activities won't bring the future that their investors demand.

Once a person takes the path toward a breakthrough, there's no turning back. It reminds me of the old World War I lyric, "How ya gonna keep 'em down on the farm after they've seen Paree?" Seeing

Paris certainly changed the doughboys and gave them a more cosmopolitan outlook than they had in the fields of Iowa. So it is with all humans.

Once you gain an understanding of a thing, you can't go back to misunderstanding it. Understanding changes you. Action creates understanding, because learning by experience is the most powerful education. You can avoid using your new understanding, but you will feel phony and miserable. You cannot "un-know" a thing.

Have you ever heard a catchy tune on the car radio but couldn't make out all the words? Maybe you tried hard to figure them out, asking other people or even getting on the Internet to look for the lyrics. Well, whether through intense listening, repetition, or research, the day comes when you finally figure out the words. Every time you hear the song again, you'll know what it is saying. You have crossed a line and can't go back.

So it is with the "knowing" that comes through the dramatic action you take toward being what you want to be someday. It's fun and exhilarating, and once you begin, you can never go back again. You have grown beyond your original limits. Only more action will satisfy you. You've seen Paris—now you want to see Rome, Bangkok, and Cairo. You can put yourself into a situation where new ideas, experiences, and actions will propel you into the future you are crying out to live.

~≈~

DISCIPLINING YOURSELF

Self-imposed discipline frees a company to do the big things that produce lifetime payoffs. In your own life, as well, you will find that habitual discipline frees your energy for your big goals.

A company will put in place financial controls and detailed procedures for decision-making and resource allocation. Although they might seem like an annoying group of rubrics, these rules keep all parts of the company working in concert with one another. These self-imposed acts of discipline actually free the company from mundane and repetitive details and liberate it to focus on the strategic initiatives that will make a real difference in the market.

The same is true for human beings. Doing what we already know we need to do frees our minds to scan the universe for potential and keeps us in shape to grab an opportunity when we see it.

The better firms don't wait until a crisis hits before they take the remedial action needed, and as an individual, you shouldn't either. Instead take constructive action toward a better future long before the fan gets hit. To do so, you've got to structure your time so that all the little things don't get in the way of your goals and objectives. The superwoman mother/professional has to learn to live with dirty dishes in the sink every once in awhile. The busy author has to ignore the annoying leaky faucet until the book is done.

This may seem just the opposite of the common concept of discipline—but contrary to popular opinion, discipline doesn't mean that every little detail is accomplished perfectly. What it does mean is that a person attends to what is truly important in his life . . . he doesn't let himself be distracted by life's trivialities. We must stop thinking that every little task needs our attention now, or we'll wake up someday to discover we haven't achieved what we wanted in life.

One thing to avoid is excessive daydreaming about the rewards you hope are ahead. Your main job is to focus on the *process* of success rather than the end goal. Boards of directors don't sit around dreaming about the new paneling they will install in the boardroom if the budget is met.

Individuals, however, often focus on the rewards of success instead of the road they need to take there. They dream about a fancy car or mansion, instead of enjoying the thrill of working on a project that is motivating, challenging, and rewarding. This is backward. If a business is to achieve success, it must commit to understanding and serving its customers and display an upbeat enthusiasm to outperform the competition. That's the process. Once success has been earned in that way, the boardroom can be paneled with mahogany and the company can lease itself a Learjet. And the same principles apply to individuals.

Often you see young people foolishly frustrating themselves by poring over the pages of *Architectural Digest, Southern Living,* or *Metropolitan Home.* Already, they are mentally committing to spending their first sixteen years of wages on costly furnishings and surroundings, and yet they feel stymied because the fruits of success are not yet ripe for them to pick! The smart up-and-comers enjoy reading *The Wall Street Journal, U.S. News,* and a variety of professional periodicals in their industry. These people are having fun learning what it takes to achieve the success that is so elusive to their frustrated peers who peer through the window of their local Crate and Barrel and lust after the latest accoutrements.

When we enjoy the process of success, rewards are much more likely! Every ballplayer knows not to divert his attention from the play in order to check the scoreboard. That's where the results are recorded—but to make the results go his way, he gives all his energy to focusing on the game. The smartest competitors don't just grind it out on the gridiron, trading hit for hit. They do like Knute Rockne did and invent the forward pass! This is the type of orbit-changing innovation that happens when you love the game and spend your time thinking about it (instead of what color you're going to paint

Mrs. Rockne's living room after the game). It takes discipline built on passion and a commitment to excellence.

The better companies know they need to find a game they love and dive into it with abandon. Do what you love so you can love what you do. And if you do both, you'll be the first to think of a new way to play the game that will turn the other players on their ears! Focused companies and single-minded individuals who lock their attention on the road ahead are the ones who uncover the big breakthroughs and end up making a real difference.

When you commit yourself to a discipline of excellence, whatever shallow goal may have motivated you originally—money, prestige, or fame—ends up not mattering at all. You'll be having too much fun on the road to be fixated on your destination. When you love what you do, you're excited to find ways to turbocharge it into the next dimension.

That's what Bill Gates did. He is passionate about his company, Microsoft. He's not just working on software; he's working on the process through which people can solve their problems using technology. Guys like that roam around listening to the market and noticing its little quirks. As a result, they discover both problems and opportunities. After they make these discoveries, they run back to the office and talk about them and think about them, and eventually they fix not only what is wrong with the product, they design something that totally leapfrogs it. That's the discipline they practice every day. And it shows.

We don't become the top guy by trying to become top guy. We do so by taking care of our constituents better than anyone else expects, surprising people with the degree of attention and service we give them, and by constantly innovating. The good news is that company after company has proven that the most important variables of success aren't the ones that require huge talent or intelligence. We must follow the golden rule and treat others as we would like to be treated. We should surprise the market with new ideas that leapfrog the current offerings, and we should outwit our competition by refusing to produce something only a little better than its predecessor.

This is easy stuff. Every grandmother knows how to make each visit a little more special for the little ones. Every grandmother knows that each of her precious grandchildren is unique, and there are no "one size fits all" solutions. Each loving act is tailored to hit its mark and resonate with the child. Each grandchild is cherished unconditionally, respected, and listened to—like no one else can—with wisdom, empathy, and a trusting spirit.

Good companies know how to grandmother their markets. Good people know how to grandmother others in their life. And these practices can be emulated, practiced, and honed to a fine edge by you . . . starting today.

Treat everyone with respect and dignity, while understanding that people need to be treated differently in order to be treated equally well. Realize that integrity is the basis of relationships—and these relationships, because they are the key to success, must be cared for. Know that ethics aren't a far-off ideal; they're at the core of profitability because they allow people to interact with one another without fanfare or compunction. These practices aren't complicated—they simply take discipline.

Companies discipline themselves to do what's in their best interest. They try new things to remain relevant, but they test their way into them, so the company won't lose a bundle if the new venture is a mistake. They work for years to come up with the big idea, then jump in with both feet when the moment arrives. But they don't jump unless all their systems are in place, and they keep doing their push-ups every day so they're ready to grab the next opportunity when it comes along. They don't over commit and fail. They don't undersell themselves and feel unfulfilled.

The best practices at the best companies tell us to listen proactively, find ways to encourage people to criticize what we're doing, and make changes before it's too late. Good companies work hard, putting in overtime and adding shifts when it will help the customer. They exceed expectations. They make allowances for intuition even in the face of copious analysis. They are open to moments of "serendipity" and struggle not to crush an ambiguous situation too quickly, lest good ideas get squelched in the process.

The better companies know what they do well and they love doing it. They don't always play by the rules as they have been laid down by the founders of the industry. They know that they need to toot their own horn, but they aren't obnoxious about it. They let their customers know when they have something that would improve the quality of the customer's life.

Their constant practice of these disciplines pays off.

～⚮～

USING YOUR RESOURCES WISELY

Successful companies storehouse resources to build the future. Likewise, if you want to achieve future goals, you must use today's resources wisely.

Too many of us are so busy earning a living that we don't have time to capitalize on the ideas we have for changing our life's orbit. For a firm to grow, it must first make a profit and retain some earnings. For a person to grow—to earn an advanced degree, for example— she must have at least a small surplus of time, talent, and money. Otherwise the would-be graduate would be so consumed by survival activities that she will have no time to pursue an education. Progress can be made only when a surplus of a resource can be tapped and focused on a purpose.

For a company, it's better to spend money on research and development toward a new, exciting product that meets the customers' needs than it is to buy ads to persuade them the revised version of an old product is really new and improved, tastes great, and is less filling. The same is true of individuals. Instead of spending a lot of money to market yourself or improve your image, spend the time and effort to really develop yourself in a way that is valuable to your future.

Companies formulate goals to help them decide where to put their resources, including people and cash. And the best firms are committed to the fine arts of following through, following up, and being persistent—all of which sound as common as apple pie . . . except just think about it, how long has it been since you had a really great piece of apple pie?

Living with long-term objectives in mind is a good way for companies to guide their allocation of resources. They don't overspend, rewarding themselves for today's performance. Companies know that life is full of surprises and they better have Plan B and maybe even Plan C ready at all times. Businesses hold fire drills in their buildings and check the tires in company vehicles as a matter of policy. They anticipate what could go wrong and have resources set aside to deal with it if it does.

Even amid the unimaginable horror of the terrorist attacks in September 2001, with their devastating impact on thousands of lives and scores of companies, well-prepared firms activated their emergency plans to keep themselves in operation. *The Wall Street Journal*, right across the street from the World Trade Center towers, moved reporters and editors to a backup facility in New Jersey and got the paper out on schedule the next morning. Employees of the bond-trading firm Cantor Fitzgerald, who had watched on television and even listened by speakerphone as hundreds of colleagues died, carried on essential tasks from other offices around the world—determined, as their chief executive said, to keep the company going in order to provide for the families of those who had perished.

The best companies know they have the resources on hand that will allow them to roll with even the most devastating punches. They have brainstormed all the things that could go wrong, and they are confident they have sufficient resources to compensate for those issues. America's finest companies are turned on by a challenge, and they meet it with as little risk to the mother ship as possible.

—☙—

ASSUMING SUCCESS

The finest, most impeccably managed companies in the country operate with one more trait: the assumption of success. Make the same assumption in your own life.

Great companies smell success in the air, and they expect it. Their day-to-day conversation fills the office with an air of anticipation. They have done their homework without falling victim to hubris. They know their mission. They are confident in their training, testing, and research. They have done the work to develop the best people and offerings on the market. They know what they will do if they hit a snag, and they go out into the world with their confidence and resilience intact. They know that success begets success and that they are part of a long line of people who have produced things of value and passed along their knowledge of what to do and not to do. So they go out there with the expectation of success as well as the charm, guts, and fervor to make something happen. They go out confident in their plan.

And you can, too. Follow the trailblazers of America's best companies. Reread the business practices I have catalogued in this book and take them to heart. You owe it to yourself. You owe it to the world.

You can manage your roles and responsibilities in such a way that your goals need never be mere fantasies again. You have the knowledge to execute your plan with strategies that are both time-tested and tailored just for you.

> OUR VISIONS OF A BETTER FUTURE ARE REAL; DREAMS DO COME TRUE; WITHOUT THAT POSSIBILITY, NATURE WOULD NOT INCITE US TO HAVE THEM.
> —JOHN UPDIKE

All you have to supply is the commitment. Once you complete the plan for your life, you'll be a bit like Moses coming down from the mountain with the Ten Commandments. He had an impeccable plan for the Hebrew nation (and humanity in general). Now human beings had to live it.

When you are ready to step forth with your plan, you'll be light-headed from your lofty thoughts up on the mountain. You may think you can walk right into the Promised Land. But it is not quite that easy. What you'll have is a roadmap to success. It's up to you to use it. Don't spend forty years wandering the desert, and don't end your life with the pain of knowing you could have done more. Commit to finding your very best self. You have many roles in life—and in each one you can become the really amazing person you want to be.

When you mean business about yourself get out your roadmap and begin taking the steps in the marvelous journey that will change your life. You'll be following the path of many great leaders, past and present. Get out there. Go. Wonders await you when *you mean business.*

Look back through the business practices catalogued in this book. Pick one that particularly pulls at your heart and your intellect, one that challenges you to change the way you mind your own business. Now look at this successful practice in light of chapter ten's key points:

- *Can you find an entirely new approach that will make this practice real in your life?*

- *How does fear hold you back from living out this practice?*

- *If you were the person you hope to be in the future, what decisions would you make pertaining to this practice? How can the person you are today follow through on those decisions?*

- *What habitual disciplines would support this practice in your life?*

- *How can you use your resources wisely to ensure that this practice becomes a reality in your life?*

- *If you knew you couldn't fail, how would you act? Go ahead . . . assume you will be successful!*